Culture and Customs of the Arab Gulf States

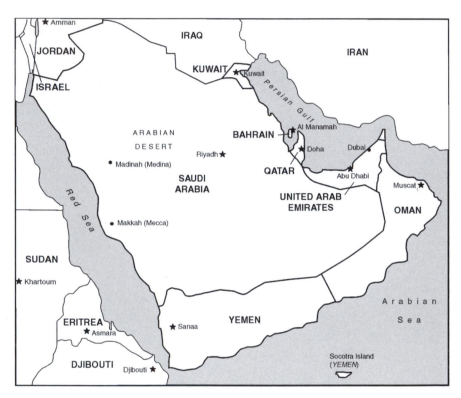

The Arab Gulf States. Courtesy of Bookcomp, Inc.

Culture and Customs of the Arab Gulf States

**REBECCA L. TORSTRICK
AND ELIZABETH FAIER**

Culture and Customs of the Middle East

GREENWOOD PRESS
Westport, Connecticut • London

Library of Congress Cataloging-in-Publication Data

Torstrick, Rebecca L., 1954–
    Culture and customs of the Arab Gulf States / Rebecca L. Torstrick and Elizabeth Faier.
        p.   cm. — (Culture and customs of the Middle East, ISSN 1550–1310)
    Includes bibliographical references and index.
    ISBN 978–0–313–33659–1 (alk. paper)
    1. Ethnology—Persian Gulf States.   2. Persian Gulf States—Social life and customs.   I. Faier,
Elizabeth, 1965–   II. Title.
    GN640.T67   2009
    306.09536—dc22   2008037871

British Library Cataloguing in Publication Data is available.

Library of Congress Catalog Card Number: 2008037871
ISBN: 978–0–313–33659–1
ISSN: 1550–1310

First published in 2009

Greenwood Press, 88 Post Road West, Westport, CT 06881
An imprint of Greenwood Publishing Group, Inc.
www.greenwood.com

Printed in the United States of America

The paper used in this book complies with the
Permanent Paper Standard issued by the National
Information Standards Organization (Z39.48–1984).

10 9 8 7 6 5 4 3 2 1

Contents

Series Foreword

AT LAST! CULTURE and Customs of the Middle East fills a deep void in reference literature by providing substantial individual volumes on crucial countries in the explosive region. The series is available at a critical juncture, with, among other events, the recent war on Iraq, the continued wrangling by U.S. interests for control of regional oil resources, the quest for Palestinian independence, and the spread of religious fundamentalist violence and repression. The authoritative, objective, and engaging cultural overviews complement and balance the volley of news bites.

As with the other Culture and Customs series, the narrative focus is on contemporary culture and life, in a historical context. Each volume is written for students and general readers by a country expert. Contents include:

Chronology
Context, including land, people, and brief historical overview
Religion and world view
Literature
Media
Cinema
Art and architecture/housing
Cuisine and dress
Gender, marriage, and family
Social customs and lifestyle
Music and dance

Preface

IN THE NINETEENTH century, the Arab Gulf steeped the imagination of the west, conjuring up exotic images of Bedouin nomads, fabulous pearls, spices and incense, and seagoing ships manned by "pirates." For the British, presence in the Arab Gulf was a necessity, serving the needs of Empire in the maintenance of trade routes with India and other countries in south Asia. In the early twentieth century, major changes were on the horizon not only in the ways people thought about the Gulf but also within local economies. By the 1930s, the Gulf pearling industry was phasing out as cultured pearls entered the market from Asia. A few decades later, the discovery of oil and natural gas brought new wealth, seeded the development of nation-states, and signaled changes to come including independence, rapid urbanization, and the establishment of ruling families. Quickly, new images of oil and oil rigs supplanted previously dominant Western ideas about these countries. With the diminution of British power, American activity grew, driven first by economic imperatives, and only later by strategic and political interests. During the Cold War years, American policymakers maintained close ties with Gulf countries in order to protect American access to the region's oil wealth. With the founding of the Arab states, Western expatriates began to move to the region, working for oil countries and aiding in the development of the new states. The 1990–91 Persian Gulf War brought the Gulf to the couches of Americans through media outlets, but the overall cultural and political ignorance about this part of the world was striking. Even today, in 2008, the nations of the Arab Gulf still call forth for Americans images that are common Western stereotypes of all Arab peoples—oil sheikhs, Bedouin nomads, veiled women, tent-dwellers. However, as this book will demonstrate, these stereotypes are a far cry from the real developments in the region—fabulous architecture, rapid social change and economic growth, and a flowering of cultural forms—all facilitated by the great wealth realized from the petroleum industry.

This book seeks to explode those stereotypical ideas about the Arab Gulf countries by introducing the reader to the richness and diversity of life in these countries. The Arab Gulf nations for centuries have been a crossroads where the peoples and cultures of India, Africa, Persia, and Arabia have met and mingled. This has created a unique hybrid culture in the region, often referred to as *khaleej*. Given the often harsh climate and arid conditions, the peoples of the region coped, surviving through the nomadic and seafaring lifestyles that took root and flourished. Today, with the vast oil wealth of the region, Arab Gulf governments are overcoming the environmental constraints and creating modern paradises in the desert. In each country, indigenous residents struggle to preserve their traditions and identities in the face of massive changes and modern consumer lifestyles. The influx of large numbers of foreign workers into the booming economies of the region also place additional strains on preserving local identity. Questions around what the Arabian Gulf will be for local and expatriate populations as well as the global economy inform debates on identity, government policy, and transnational corporate development. In response to the rich history of the region as well as the fast pace of political, economic, and cultural development, the rulers of each country have sought unique ways to establish what modern Islamic states should look like both internally and to the world. The challenge of embracing Western-style economic development through globalization while preserving Gulf traditions is evident in all facets of life.

Chronology

50,000 years ago	Humans inhabit Qatar, building camps and settlements along the coast and working flint.
ca. 5000 BC	Pottery found in Qatar from the al-Ubaid culture of Mesopotamia.
ca. 4000–2000 BC	Dilmun culture flourishes on Bahrain Island.
1800 BC	Dilmun begins to decline.
seventh century BC	Assyrians control the Gulf region.
325 BC	Alexander the Great begins his exploration of the Gulf.
250 BC	Parthians control the Gulf and Oman.
third century AD	Sassanians control the Gulf and establish colonies in Oman.
610 AD	Muhammad begins to preach his revelations.
700s	Islam introduced in Oman.
800s	Ibadi sect in Oman begins rule by succession.
1508	Portuguese establish colonial presence in Oman.
sixteenth century	Portuguese invade Bahrain.
1517–1538	Portuguese rule Qatar, until defeated by the Ottomans.
1600s	Northeast part of Arab Gulf becomes part of Ottoman Empire.

1602	Bahraini uprising against Portuguese.
1624–1744	Ya'aruba dynasty in Oman.
1650	Yarubid Imamate of Oman recaptures Muscat from the Portuguese.
about 1700	Bani Yas tribes establish themselves at Abu Dhabi.
1739	Persians invade Oman.
1742	Ahmad ibn Said al-Said and his family expel Iranians from Oman and take control of the coast.
1749	Ahmad ibn Said al-Said is named imam in Oman.
1756	Al-Sabah family gains control of what will become Kuwait.
1760s	Al-Khalifa and al-Jalahima sections of the Bani Utub migrate to Qatar's northwest coast and found Az Zubarah.
1783	Bani Utub of Kuwait and Qatar capture Bahrain.
	Persians expelled from Bahrain; al-Khalifa family arrives.
early 1800s	Bani Utub move from central Arabia into the northern Gulf; the al-Sabah family establishes itself as leaders in what will become modern Kuwait; the al-Khalifa are established in what is now Bahrain.
1800s–1900s	Omani empire expands to Zanzibar and parts of Indian subcontinent.
1820	Great Britain signs treaty with the al-Qasimi tribes who control Ras al-Khaymah, Ajman, and Sharjah. They also have a treaty with Dubai (Bani Yas tribes) and Bahrain (al-Khalifa tribes).
1835	Abu Dhabi signs treaty with Great Britain.
1853	Great Britain and the seven Trucial coast states sign the Treaty of Maritime Peace in Perpetuity, which gives Great Britain power over foreign affairs.
1861	Bahrain signs treaty with Britain; Britain grants protection from Ottomans in exchange for complete access to the Gulf.
	Zanzibar declared independent sultanate.
1899	Kuwait signs treaty with Great Britain.
1913	Ottomans renounce rule over Qatar.
	Ruling of Oman divided between Ibadi imams in interior regions and the sultan in coastal areas.

Bahrain signs treaty with Great Britain but remains under British administration.

1916   Qatar signs treaty with Great Britain.

1920s–1930s   Pearling industry declines quickly in the region due to the Japanese development of the process of making cultured pearls.

1932   Oil discovered in Bahrain.

                    Sultan Said bin Taimur comes to power in Oman.

1935   British naval base moved to Bahrain.

1938   Oil discovered in Kuwait.

1939   Oil discovered in Qatar.

1952   Seven Emirates in the United Arab Emirates form the Trucial Council.

1959   Sultan Said gains control over interior of Oman from Ibadi imams.

1960   Oil discovered in Abu Dhabi.

1961   Sheikh Isa bin Salman al-Khalifa installed as ruler of Bahrain.

June 19   Independence for Kuwait.

1962   Oil discovered in Oman.

1963   National Assembly elections held in Kuwait.

1965–1975   Dhofar rebellion in Oman eventually leads to bloodless coup by Qaboos against his father, Sheikh Said.

1966   Oil discovered in Dubai.

1968   Bahrain and Qatar join Trucial states.

1970   Sultan Qaboos bin Said assumes power in Oman.

1971

August 15   Independence for Bahrain.

September 3   Independence for Qatar.

December 2   Independence for the United Arab Emirates.

1972   Ras al-Khaimah joins the United Arab Emirates.

                    Khalifa bin Hamad al-Thani comes to power after coup.

                    Males vote in Bahraini election for Constituent Assembly.

1973	Oil discovered in Sharjah.
1975	National Assembly dissolved in Bahrain.
1976	National Assembly dissolved in Kuwait.
1981	Bahrain, Kuwait, Oman, Qatar, Saudi Arabia, and the United Arab Emirates form the Gulf Cooperation Council.
1984	Oil discovered in Ras al-Khaymah.
1985	Deportation of Iranians from Kuwait.
1986	King Fahd causeway opens between Bahrain and Saudi Arabia.
1990	
August 2	Iraq invades Kuwait.
August 6	Iraq annexes Kuwait.
1991	Bahrain signs defense cooperation agreement with United States.
February 28	Coalition forces liberate Kuwait; Iraqis are forced out.
1992	Bahrain Shura Consultative Council appointed by emir.
1994	Iraq recognizes Kuwait's independence.
1995	Hamad bin Khalifa al-Thani comes to power in Qatar after deposing his father in bloodless coup.
	Bahrain cabinet includes five Shia ministers.
1996	Al-Jazeera television station begins operation in Qatar.
1997	Sultan Qaboos extends vote and participation to women in Consultative Council (Majlis al-Shura) of Oman.
1999	Democraticization begins in Qatar with municipal elections.
	Sheikh Isa of Bahrain dies; his son Sheikh Hamad becomes emir.
2000	Sheikh Hamad appoints non-Muslims (one Christian and one Jew) and women to Shura Consultative Council.
2001	Bahrainis vote for constitutional monarchy.
2002	Limited parliamentary elections held in Bahrain, with women having the right to stand for positions.
	Voting granted to all Omanis over twenty-one years of age.
2003	Qatar approves a new constitution that establishes a parliament.

Sheikha Ahmad al-Mahmoud appointed first female Qatari and first Gulf state minister.

2004   Sheikh Zayed bin Sultan al-Nahyan, president of the United Arab Emirates, dies; his son Sheikh Khalifa bin Zayed al-Nahyan succeeds him.

Rawiyah bint Saud al-Busaidiyah appointed first female minister (with portfolio) in Oman following Sheikha Aisha bint Khalfan bin Jameel al-Sayabiyah's appointment in 2003 (rank of minister but no portfolio).

Sheikha Lubna Khalid al-Qasimi appointed first female minister in United Arab Emirates.

Nada Haffadh appointed first female minister in Bahrain.

2005   Women receive vote in Kuwait; Massouma al-Mubarak appointed first female minister.

2006   Sheikh Maktoum bin Rashid al-Maktoum, ruler of Dubai, dies; Sheikh Mohammed bin Rashid al-Maktoum succeeds him.

Sheikh Jaber, emir of Kuwait, dies and is succeeded by Sheikh Saad, who is quickly removed for medical reasons. Sheikh Sabah al-Ahmad becomes emir.

First national elections (Federal National Council) held in United Arab Emirates; only appointed individuals can vote.

Shias in Bahrain gain 40 percent of votes in general election.

2007   Government in Kuwait resigns; new cabinet appointees include two women.

Cyclone Gonu wreaks havoc in Oman; 50 people are killed.

2008   Parliament dissolved in Kuwait, after which elections see Islamist gains and no women in new cabinet.

1

Land, People, and History

IN FEBRUARY 2006, Dubai Ports World (DPW), a company owned by the government of Dubai in the United Arab Emirates (UAE), purchased the British firm Peninsular and Oriental Steam Navigation Company (P&O), which held leases to manage a number of ports in the United States. After the purchase, the U.S. Treasury Department reviewed the leases and approved their transfer to DPW. However, by the end of that month, the economic transaction had become the focal point of congressional investigations and actions, as many Americans questioned whether a foreign firm could be trusted to protect America's national security. It did not matter that President Bush himself supported DPW or that the UAE has been a firm American ally. By March 9, 2006, DPW announced that it would sell the American port leases to an American firm. It completed that transaction on March 16, 2007, when the American insurance company American International Group acquired 100 percent of the P&O shares.

The real heart of the controversy was not whether a foreign firm could provide adequate security—the previous owners of the leases were, after all, British. The controversy swirled around whether an *Arab* firm could be trusted, bringing to light the stereotypes and prejudices many Americans continue to hold about the Arab world.[1] When Americans think about the Arab Gulf states, they may envision images of scantily clad, veiled women living in harems; Bedouin men on camels traversing endless sand dunes; and wealthy oil sheikhs who hold the power of life and death over their populations. Not only are such images wildly inaccurate, but they obscure the cultural richness and diversity of this region, where Arab, Persian, Indian, and African peoples and cultures have mixed and merged over countless decades. Hence we begin this chapter by providing a brief overview of the geography, people, and history of this vital, dynamic region.

THE LAND

The Arab Gulf states can be found on the western shore of the Arabian Gulf, mainly at the tip of the Arabian Peninsula, except for Kuwait, which is sandwiched between Saudi Arabia and Iraq at the northernmost part of the Gulf. Facing these states across the Gulf is Iran, which explains why the Arabian Gulf is also known as the Persian Gulf. The Arabian Peninsula is believed to have split from a larger landmass that included Africa. As Arabia moved away, the western side rose, while the eastern side fell, creating the Arabian Gulf. The waters of the Gulf allowed the residents of the peninsula to create a vibrant trading network between the area of the Tigris-Euphrates and the Indian subcontinent.

Bahrain is an archipelago of thirty-three islands, the largest of which, Bahrain Island (about 221 square miles), is 83 percent of the total area of the country. Bahrain is about fifteen miles from the Saudi coast and seventeen miles from Qatar. The islands are linked together by causeways and bridges. Al-Muharraq, the second largest island (3.7 miles long), is the site of the country's international airport. Other islands (Jazirat al-Azl, Sitrah) are the sites of export terminals, ship repair facilities, and dry docks. Bahrain is linked to the Saudi coastline through the island of Umm An Nasan (the emir's private property). The island of Nabi Salah is important for its freshwater springs, which help the island grow date palms. Jiddah is the site of the prison. Bahrain and Qatar have been involved in a dispute over the Hawar Islands, which are under Bahrain's sovereignty but are located only 0.8 miles off the Qatari coast (but almost 12.5 miles away from Bahrain).

Bahrain Island is largely a low-lying desert, with rolling hills and shallow ravines. Its oil fields are in the center of Bahrain Island, and Bahrain also gets oil from offshore fields in the Gulf. Along the northern coast, a three-mile-wide strip of fertile land supports agriculture. The highest point on the island is Jabal ad Dukhan (Mountain of Smoke), which rises 440 feet. This area is also the site of most of the island's oil wells. The capital, Manama, is located at the northern tip of the island. Mina Salman is a major port city also located on the island, while the second largest city, al-Muharraq, is located on the nearby island of the same name. Most of the settlements on Bahrain Island are in the northern part of the country.

Kuwait occupies a triangular wedge of territory (about 6,879 square miles) that borders Saudi Arabia, Iraq, and the Gulf. Kuwait's coastline extends for 121 miles. Its border with Saudi Arabia is 155 miles long, while its northern border with Iraq, 149 miles long, has been the source of disputes. Besides land on the Arabian Peninsula, Kuwait also controls nine islands in the Gulf, two of which, Bubiyan and Warbah, are strategically important because they are located at the mouth of the Euphrates River. Iraq has sought to gain control over these two islands. In fact, Saddam Hussein used claims over these islands as his excuse for his 1990 invasion of Kuwait.

Kuwait's terrain is mainly flat, with a gravelly desert. Its principal oil fields lie in the south, below a limestone dome that lies beneath the surface. The western border of the country is formed by the Wadi al-Batin, a wide valley. The twenty-five miles of Kuwait Bay provide a natural, sheltered harbor for shipping. Kuwait City, the capital, is located on this bay and is the largest city. Al-Jahrah, nearby and slightly inland, is the next largest city. Most of Kuwait's settlements are found along the coastline. The island of Faylakah in the Gulf near Kuwait Bay was highly populated prior to the Gulf War. However, Faylakah was turned into an Iraqi military area during the 1990 conflict, and its residents were evicted. After the war's end, the island was taken over for use as a military zone. Settlements there served as staging grounds for specialized urban warfare training for American forces prior to the invasion of Iraq in 2003.

Kuwait City at night. Courtesy of Dave Hutton.

Village in Musandam Peninsula wadi, Oman. Courtesy of Elizabeth Faier.

Oman, the largest of the Gulf states, extends along the coast of the Gulf of Oman and the Arabian Sea. It covers over 115,830 square miles and borders Saudi Arabia, the UAE on its west, and Yemen to the south. Part of Oman's territory, the Ru'us al-Jibal (northern tip of the Musandam Peninsula), is separated from the rest of Oman by a fifty-mile corridor of the UAE. Oman includes mountain ranges, coastal plains, and desert. The Rub al-Khali (or "Empty Quarter") of Saudi Arabia forms part of its western border, isolating it from any contact from this direction and forcing the country to rely on the sea for its connections to the rest of the world.

Oman can be divided into three regions: the Ru'us al-Jibal, Oman proper, and Dhofar. The Ru'us al-Jibal area consists of low mountains, part of the northernmost tip of the western al-Hajar Mountains. Khawr ash Shamm and Ghubbat al-Shazirah are two inlets along the coastline, and the Khawr ash Shamm, with its rugged, steep cliffs, has been compared to a Norwegian fjord. Oman proper consists of the narrow al-Batinah coastal plain on the north coast, once one reenters Oman from the UAE, and the parallel chain of the al-Hajar Mountains. The mountains form two ranges, an eastern one and a western one, divided by Wadi Samail, a valley that runs from Muscat into the interior. The high ridge of the range, al-Jabal al-Akhdar, rises to more than 9,842 feet in places. Beyond the mountains, one enters a dry gravel plain called al-Zahirah that blends into the Rub al-Khali and, eventually, inner Oman. Additional desert plains extend to the south. The southern region of Dhofar also has a parallel structure of coastal plains, mountains (the Qara Mountains), and interior desert.

Oman's major city and capital is Muscat, in the north of the country along the coast. Muscat and nearby Matrah both have natural harbors that provide safe anchorage for ships. The largest city in the al-Batinah plain is Sohar, while Salalah, near the border with Yemen, is the major center for the Dhofar region. Nizwa, in the hills of al-Jabal al-Akhdar, is another major population center.

Qatar shares a border with Saudi Arabia and the UAE. Located on a peninsula that juts into the Arabian Gulf from the Arabian Peninsula, Qatar covers 4,430 square miles. The peninsula is flat and rocky, with its highest point rising only 338 feet. Massive sand dunes surround Khawr al-Udayd, an inlet of the Arabian Gulf in the southeast, near the UAE (and the site of another border dispute). The Dukhan oil field lies on the west coast, under limestone formations. Qatar's capital, Doha, is located centrally on the eastern coast and is one of the two ports capable of handling commercial shipping. Other important port cities include Umm Said (the other commercial port), al-Khawr, and al-Wakra, all located along the eastern coast. Navigation is possible only where channels have been dredged because of shallow waters and the presence of coral reefs offshore. The capital Doha is linked to other settlements on the island by a network of paved roads (about one thousand kilometers total). Most settlements are found along the coastlines, but there are a few in the interior of the peninsula.

The UAE is a federation of seven separate emirates joined together to form a single country that covers about thirty thousand square miles. It shares a border with Qatar on the northwest, a border with Saudi Arabia (329 miles) on the west and south, and a border with Oman (280 miles) on the east. Its coastline on the southern shore of the Arabian Gulf stretches for more than 870 miles. The individual emirates include Abu Dhabi, Ajman, al-Fujayrah, Dubai, Ras al-Khaymah, Sharjah, and Umm al-Qaywayn. Abu Dhabi (the northernmost emirate on the coast) occupies most of the land area (87 percent). Dubai, located next to Abu Dhabi, composes less than 5 percent, with Sharjah, the next emirate moving south along the coast, composing a bit more than 3 percent. The remaining four emirates occupy 5 percent altogether; Umm al-Qaywayn and Ras al-Khaymah are located moving south along the coastline to the border, with the Ru'us al-Jibal area of Oman and al-Fujayrah and Ajman located in the strip of land that separates Ru'us al-Jibal from the rest of Oman. Ras al-Khaymah lays claim to a large portion of land in the southwest of this territory, Sharjah claims a piece along the Gulf of Oman and in the interior, and Dubai lays claim to a small piece of land that borders Oman. There are pockets of Oman inside the UAE, near Hatta.

Sand dunes on edge of empty quarter, Abu Dhabi Emirate, UAE. Courtesy of Elizabeth Faier.

The UAE encompasses a flat coastal plain (part of the al-Batinah plain), portions of the al-Hajar Mountains, an interior desert that joins the Rub al-Khali of Saudi Arabia, and an elevated plateau. The mountains separate the al-Batinah coast from the rest of the country. Harbors exist at Diba al-Hisn, Kalba, and Khawr Fakkan on the Gulf of Oman and at Dubai, Abu Dhabi, and Sharjah on the Gulf coast. Salt pans (*sabkha*) run along most of the Gulf coast, extending into the interior. In Abu Dhabi's desert area, there are two oases with enough underground water to handle cultivation and settlements: the Liwa oasis (south near the Saudi border) and the al-Buraymi oasis (northeast on the Abu Dhabi–Oman border). More than 80 percent of the oil in the UAE is located in Abu Dhabi. Dubai, Sharjah, and Ras al-Khaymah account for the remainder of the country's oil production.

The largest city, Dubai, is the UAE's main port and center of commerce. Abu Dhabi, the second largest city, is the federal capital. Sharjah, Ajman, and Ras al-Khaymah represent other large population centers, all along the coast. At the al-Buraymi oasis, the town of al-Ayn represents the largest population center in the interior.

The climate in the Arab Gulf states can be broken into roughly two periods: hot, dry, or humid summers and moderate winters. Summer generally begins in April and lasts until October. Across the region, temperatures top the 100-degree-Fahrenheit mark, ranging from 107 to 115 degrees in Kuwait and 104 to 118 degrees in Bahrain, and topping 104 degrees in Qatar, 118 degrees in the UAE, and 122 degrees in Oman in the interior (in the shade). Coastal areas may see slightly lower temperatures. In Muscat, Oman, for example, highs are more in the range of the low nineties, but if a *gharbi* (a western wind

Sabkha (salt flats), Abu Dhabi Emirate, UAE. Courtesy of Elizabeth Faier.

that comes from the Rub al-Khali) is blowing, it can raise the temperature by another ten to eighteen degrees Fahrenheit. Kuwaitis deal with sandstorms during June and July, as do residents of Qatar and the UAE throughout the spring and summer. In Bahrain, sandstorms take the form of the *qaws*, a hot, dry, southwesterly wind that blows sand everywhere. Qatari citizens have alternating periods of dryness and intense humidity. In the UAE, the *sharqi*, a humid, southeasterly wind, will punctuate the late summer. Residents of the al-Batinah plain of Oman see lower temperatures than do residents of the interior, but they also experience 90 percent humidity. The mountain areas of both the UAE and Oman are much cooler. The Dhofar region of Oman varies in its climate: from June to September, it has a monsoon climate and gets cool winds from the Indian Ocean.

Winter in the region begins in October or November and lasts until March or mid-April. Winter temperatures are quite moderate, ranging in degrees Fahrenheit from the fifties to the low seventies in all the countries. In Kuwait, temperatures can drop into the upper thirties at night, but frost is rare. Winter is also the time of rain and high humidity (above 90 percent). The *shammal* in Bahrain is the southeasterly prevailing wind that brings damp air with it.

Rainfall is quite limited across the region. Kuwait averages 2.9 to 3.9 inches a year; Bahrain averages 2.8 inches; Qatar averages 3.9 inches; the UAE averages less than 4.7 inches (although it can reach as much as 13.7 inches in the mountains); and Oman's precipitation rate ranges between 0.7 and 3.9 inches along the coasts and interior (in the mountains, as much as 27.5 inches can fall in a year). It is quite common in many countries for rainfall to come in a sudden, violent thunderstorm that quickly drenches the landscape, flooding streambeds (wadis) and ravines and washing out roads.

It is clear that access to water is a key issue in all the states in this region. Bahrain has no permanent rivers or streams. Its water comes from natural springs at the north of Bahrain Island and other nearby islands. There are also underground freshwater deposits beneath the Gulf of Bahrain that extend to the Saudi Arabian coast. Bahrain built desalination plants, which, since the 1980s, have provided about 60 percent of the water consumed by the population. Qatar has limited underground water, and what water there is has a high mineral content that makes it unsuitable for drinking or irrigation use. Here, too, most water needed for consumption is provided by desalination plants. Kuwait relies on water from a freshwater aquifer (discovered in 1960) on the western side of the Ar Rawdatayn formation in the north of the country and on another aquifer near Kuwait City, in the Ash Shuaybah field. Water from the latter source, however, is brackish, unlike the water from the north. Distilled water fills most of the country's needs. In the UAE, Abu Dhabi's

Liwa oasis, Abu Dhabi Emirate, UAE. Courtesy of Elizabeth Faier.

desert area has underground water at two oases—Liwa and al-Buraymi—which makes it possible for people to settle permanently there and cultivate crops. Historically, people used shallow, hand-dug wells to tap into groundwater and captured water from the limited rainfall. Today, most of the water needed in the UAE is produced by desalination plants. There are no rivers. Masafi is the most popular bottled water in the Gulf region and comes from the natural springs in the village of the same name, on the edge of the al-Hajar Mountains. In Oman, the al-Jabal al-Akhdar plateau has a large reservoir under it that provides springs for low-lying areas. Elaborate underground canals, called *aflāj*, carry water from these underground streams to the plains. Once there, the wadi channels water to the valleys. When rainfall is adequate, this area can support agriculture. Dhofar, with its monsoon climate, sees heavier annual rainfall. As a result, it has constantly moving streams and is the most fertile area for growing crops. Salalah, with its lush growth, is a popular spot to which people flock in the summer.

Most of the animal species that live in the region thrive in desert conditions. These include the Arabian oryx (Qatar's national animal), various gazelles, hares, foxes, and jerboas (small jumping rodents). In the UAE, the caracal (a close relative of lynxes) and sand cat can be found. In Oman,

Hatta pools, al-Hajar al Gharbi Mountains (western mountains) in background, Dubai Emirate, UAE. Courtesy of Anders Linde-Laursen.

leopards and mountain goats, rare species, are currently protected by the government. In Bahrain, mongooses live in the irrigated areas; they were probably introduced to the country from India. Numerous snakes and lizards are native to the region, including the sand viper, monitor, dab lizard, and loggerhead turtle (another Omani protected species). Bahrain has few native birds, but it serves as a resting point for birds migrating to and from more northern latitudes. Oman has a rich variety of bird species (over 450), including several forms of ibis, the Egyptian vulture, bulbuls, sunbirds, and several cormorants. Only some birds are resident year-round; the others use Oman as a stopping point in their migrations or as a breeding location.

Given the arid conditions in the region, it might be assumed that not much grows there, but this would be far from the truth. Qatar boasts more than 130 different plant species; Bahrain has 200 different species; Kuwait accounts for almost 400 species; over 600 species are known in the UAE; and in Oman, over 1,200 species have been identified. Arid areas in all countries host low-growing shrubs and scrub. When it rains, the deserts bloom, as all

Cistanche tubulosa, mangrove, Qatar. Courtesy of Anders Linde-Laursen.

Qatar mangrove, south of al-Wakra. Courtesy of Anders Linde-Laursen.

sorts of flowers come forth. In the UAE, many trees have been planted by the government in Abu Dhabi, particularly mangrove trees. Mangrove areas can also be found in Qatar (north and south of Doha) and in al-Fujayrah. Date palms and alfalfa, or even mangos, are grown at various oases in the UAE. In Kuwait, halophytes (salt-loving plants) are found in the marshy areas. Bahrain's irrigated areas grow fruit trees, vegetables, and fodder for animals. Oman's varied climate helps explain the wide variety of species identified there, which include acacia trees; frankincense trees; date palms; flowering plants such as wild pansies, cowslip, and poinciana; and cultivated fruits, grains, and vegetables.

THE PEOPLE AND LANGUAGE

It is not possible to get exact population estimates for the Arab Gulf states. New infrastructural projects in some Gulf states, such as the development of Dubai Industrial and Dubai Waterfront in the UAE, are leading to estimates of an increased population of 2 million people in the emirate just because of these two projects. All of the countries in the region have substantial populations of noncitizen foreigners, ranging from 17 percent of Oman's population to over 80 percent of the population of the UAE. Table 1.1 contains current estimates of populations in the region, including the percentage of nonnationals included in the overall population figures. As can be seen from

Table 1.1
Population Estimates for the Arab Gulf States (as of July 2008)

Country	Total Population	Nonnationals	Percentage Nonnationals
Bahrain	718,306	235,108	33
Kuwait	2,596,799	1,291,354	49.7
Oman	3,311,640	577,293	17
Qatar	928,635	NA[a]	75[b]
United Arab Emirates	5,600,000	4,737,600	84.6

[a]Qatar does not break down its population statistics into numbers of nationals and non-nationals; some scholars say this is to disguise the large percentage of its population that is nonnational.
[b]Estimated.
Source: Central Intelligence Agency, *The World Factbook*, https://www.cia.gov/library/publications/the-world-factbook/index.html.

Table 1.1, three of the four Gulf states (Kuwait, Qatar, and the UAE) have sizable nonnational populations.

The indigenous populations of most of the countries are Arab, of tribal Bedouin origin. The emirates of UAE were the territory of the Bani Yas and al-Qawasim tribes, while the Bani Utub settled in Bahrain and Kuwait and the al-Thani in Qatar. The Bani Yas moved into the area from central Arabia around 1700, while the Qawasim were indigenous and had lived on the coast during pre-Islamic times. The Bani Utub moved from central Arabia into the northern Gulf in the early 1800s. The al-Thani, a branch of the Bani Tameem, also of central Arabian origin, arrived in the region in the eighteenth century. In addition to Arabs, the indigenous population in Bahrain and Qatar also includes people of Persian origin, and in the UAE, besides those of Persian origin, one also finds people of Baluchi or Indian descent.[2] In Oman, the same Persian-Baluchi-Indian mix can be found, but added to these are Africans, brought as slaves from the eastern African coast and Zanzibar.[3]

The nonnational population of the Gulf states includes significant numbers of other Arabs—people from Egypt, Syria, Jordan, Lebanon, and Palestine. In addition to other Arabs, one finds people from south Asia (Indians and Pakistanis), immigrants from Southeast Asia and the Philippines (many women work as domestic help), and North American and British professionals working at the universities and in other top-level jobs in regional companies. Educated Indians and Pakistanis can be found in the mid-professional levels. Many of the immigrants from south and Southeast Asia work as manual laborers in the oil and gas industries and in construction. These immigrants have come to be more favored as workers (especially over workers from other Arab countries) in recent years because they do not speak the language and are unlikely to cause problems for host governments, and they are more likely to return to their home countries.

Arabic, the official language in all countries in the region, is diglossic, meaning that it exists in two different forms. Modern Standard Arabic (MSA), which developed from the classical Arabic of the Quran, is the official literary language spoken by educated people and used on television, in newspapers, and in government deliberations. On the streets, however, people speak a dialect of Arabic known as Gulf Arabic (or Khaleeji Arabic). Gulf Arabic retains strong Bedouin characteristics. What sets it apart from other spoken dialects of Arabic and MSA is its small number of Persian loanwords as well as its differing pronunciations of certain words. Gulf Arabic distinguishes more vowel sounds than MSA. In Gulf Arabic, the /q/ sound of the letter *qaf* of MSA may be replaced by the sounds /g/ or /j/. The /k/ sound of the letter *kaf* may be replaced with a pronunciation /ch/ (*kalb*, "dog," as /chalb/), or the sound /j/ may be pronounced as /y/ (*jeeb*, "bring," as /yeeb/).

Besides Arabic, one finds a wide variety of other languages present in the Gulf countries, largely due to the high number of foreign guest workers who reside there. These include Malayalam (the language of the southern province of Kerala in India), Tamil (India and Sri Lanka), Hindi, Urdu (Pakistan), Baluchi, Filipino, Somali, Swahili, Pashto, Bengali, and Farsi (Iran) as well as English and a variety of other European languages. One song and dance tradition, the *lewa*, is sung in mingled Swahili and Arabic, reflecting its African roots. In every Gulf state, at least two newspapers appear in English.

ECONOMY

Historically, the economies of the Arab Gulf states reflected their geographies and the physical resources available in each country. Almost every country relied on the sea in some way to sustain its people. Fishing was a key economic activity in every country. With over two hundred different varieties of fish, the Gulf is rich in marine resources, and fisherman were able to catch sardines, bluefish, mackerel, shark, tuna, abalone, lobsters, and oysters, among other species. Pearl diving sustained the economies of the UAE, Qatar, Kuwait, and Bahrain until the industry crashed in the 1930s, due in part to the development of less expensive cultured pearls by the Japanese and the shock of the worldwide depression. Maritime trading activities were important in the UAE, Kuwait, and Oman. Oman had a thriving trade with Zanzibar and eastern Africa, until the British ended the slave trade in the mid-1800s and later split off Zanzibar from Oman in 1856. The Omani

Fishing harbor, al-Wakra, Qatar. Courtesy of Anders Linde-Laursen.

government was then left with very limited economic resources. The Kuwaitis were known for their shipbuilding industry, and their merchants developed long-distance trade during the off-season for pearling. Given the scarcity of water in most of the countries, agricultural production had a limited role in many Gulf states. Date production was essential in the UAE and Bahrain. In Bahrain, twenty-three different varieties of dates were grown, with enough produced for both local consumption and export. Farming in Oman has always been important. With five distinct agricultural regions (and adequate rainfall), Oman is the only Gulf state that has consistently produced a variety of crops, including apricots, grapes, peaches, walnuts, dates, barley, wheat, corn, alfalfa, and vegetables. Finally, livestock herding was a final important economic activity, especially in the UAE and Qatar.

Since the discovery of oil in the region, the economies of the Arab Gulf states have taken off (see the history section, later, for more discussion about the growth of this industry). In 2007, individual estimated gross domestic product (GDP) figures for the region were as follows: Bahrain, $24.5 billion; Kuwait, $130.1 billion; Oman, $61.61 billion; Qatar, $57.69 billion; and UAE, $167.3 billion.[4] While oil remains a significant source of wealth in the region's economies, each country is seeking to diversify. Bahrain has focused on developing its Islamic banking sector, has implemented a free trade agreement with the United States, and is a major aluminum exporter. Kuwait produces cement, has a food processing industry, and is involved in shipbuilding and repair. Oman is actively diversifying its economy because of dwindling oil revenues. It, too, has a free trade agreement with the United States and is pursuing similar arrangements with the European Union, China, and Japan. Industrial development is focusing on petrochemicals, the manufacture of metals (copper, steel), and the development of ports. In addition, Oman is seeking further revenues from tourism and to develop its higher education and information technology infrastructures. Qatar's economy is expanding due to oil and natural gas production. Fully 60 percent of its GDP is in these two sectors, the demand for which has remained high. Qatar's natural gas reserves are the third largest holdings in the world. Besides these two industries, Qatar has some agricultural production and produces cement, ammonia, and fertilizers, and the country also does commercial ship repair. The UAE has about 40 percent of its GDP in the areas of gas and oil. The transformation in the way of life has been stark, as residents went from living in a relatively impoverished area to having a high per capita income in a relatively short time span. The UAE has been actively diversifying its economy by developing tourism, airport and aviation services, facilities management, and exhibitions.

Dubai, in the UAE, represents one of the success stories in the region. Since 2000, GDP there has grown at an annual rate of 13 percent. Much of this growth has been the result of key government investments in the emirates and is not connected to oil. Internet City, Healthcare City, the Palm, and Dubailand represent specialized zones and projects developed by the government to generate revenue.[5] These specialized zones have made Dubai the destination of preference for media and Internet companies, health care services, and tourism in the region. Dubailand, currently under development, will be a city divided into seven theme worlds. When it is completed, it will be twice the size of Disney World. The goal of the project is to attract two hundred thousand daily visitors to the city, hence increasing tourism as a source of revenue for the emirate. The Palm is a development involving the creation of three uniquely shaped artificial islands; it represents the largest land reclamation project in the world. The islands contain villas and apartments, marinas, restaurants, shopping malls, water theme parks, sports facilities, health spas, luxury hotels, and beaches. In fact, the three islands will increase Dubai's beachfronts by 323 miles. Once again, the intent of these developments is to increase tourism to the emirate.

Dubai is already seeing significant tourist traffic. The emirate saw 5.1 million tourists in the first nine months of 2007, with its airport handling fully 22 percent of the passenger traffic in the Middle East. In fact, the UAE, Kuwait, Qatar, and Bahrain have all established open-sky policies to expand their share of the airport and aviation industry. Dubai has also become the foremost exhibition destination in the Middle East and Africa, making it a key player in the global events and exhibitions industry. In 2008, Dubai hosted a cable and satellite exhibition, the International Horse Fair, the Gulf Art Fair, the World Travel and Tourism conference, the World Association of Chefs congress, and an international retail real estate congress.

GOVERNMENT

Currently the Gulf states are controlled by ten ruling families: the al-Khalifa (Bahrain), the al-Sabah (Kuwait), the al-Thani (Qatar), the al-Said (Oman), and, in the UAE, the al-Nuhayyan (Abu Dhabi), the al-Nuaimi (Ajman), the al-Sharqi (al-Fujayrah), the al-Maktum (Dubai), the al-Qasimi (Ras al-Khaymah and Sharjah), and the al-Mualla (Umm al-Qaywayn). Every state has a written constitution that spells out rights and obligations of citizens as well as delineating that each country is a hereditary emirate and, in some cases, spelling out which family has the right to rule. Each country has adopted a different system of organization for its governance.

Bahrain is a constitutional monarchy, ruled by a king. The king appoints the prime minister and the cabinet. There is a two-house legislature. The Consultative Council consists of forty members, who are appointed by the king. The Chamber of Deputies consists of forty members, who are elected to serve four-year terms. The last elections for the Chamber of Deputies were in 2006. Kuwait is considered to be a constitutional emirate. There is an elected National Assembly that consists of fifty members, who also serve four-year terms. Elections in Kuwait were last held in May 2008. The emir appoints the prime minister and the deputy prime ministers, who serve on the Council of Ministers.

Oman is considered a monarchy, ruled by a sultan. There is no constitution; however, Sultan Qaboos issued a basic law in November 1996 that established a two-house legislature, provided for a prime minister (appointed by the sultan), and guaranteed basic civil liberties to citizens. Some members of the government are appointed; others are elected, as in the other states in the region. Qatar is an emirate; its constitution went into effect in 2005. There is an Advisory Council of thirty-five members, who are appointed by the emir, and a Central Municipal Council of twenty-nine members, who are elected. The last election for this body was held in 2007. According to the new constitution, the Advisory Council will undergo a transformation. It will become a forty-five-member body, with two-thirds of its members elected and one-third appointed by the emir. Preparations are currently under way for elections to this new body sometime in 2008.

The UAE represents a limited federation of the seven emirates. Unofficially, the presidency is held by the ruler of Abu Dhabi, while the ruler of Dubai serves as vice president and prime minister. The seven hereditary rulers of the separate emirates comprise the Supreme Council, which elects the Council of Ministers and appoints the forty-member Federal National Council, which reviews all proposed legislation. More recently, the Federal National Council has changed to allow half its members to be elected to two-year terms. The first elections were held in 2006. Each of the rulers of the seven emirates also retains control in certain areas over his own state.

HISTORY

Evidence from excavations in Saudi Arabia suggests that people lived in the Arabian Peninsula in Neolithic times, about eight thousand years ago. The Gulf region itself has been occupied since at least 5000 BC, putting it among the oldest continuously inhabited places on the planet. Its location at the mouth of the Tigris and Euphrates rivers gave it immense strategic importance for trade between the civilizations that developed around those rivers and other civilizations as far away as Egypt and India. Tradition has it that the fish man Oannes swam up the Gulf and brought civilized living to its inhabitants (Zahlan 1989, 1).

There is sparse evidence from the period of 5000–3000 BC of settlers along the Gulf (from Bahrain and Qatar to Oman) being in contact with the Ubaid civilization of Mesopotamia. Uruk-period (ca. 4000–3100 BC) pottery, flints, obsidian from Turkey, and seashells are found at archaeological sites located in the eastern provinces of what is now Saudi Arabia, Bahrain, Qatar, the UAE, and Oman. When the Turkish trade in copper to Mesopotamia collapsed, it is likely that the Mesopotamians looked to Oman for new sources of the ore. Out of the trade that developed in the region sprouted two major civilizations: Dilmun (eastern Arabia and what is now Bahrain) and Magan (in Oman).

Dilmun rose to power in 2800 BC and played a major role in the region for the next two thousand years. By the middle of the third millennium, Bahrain had a flourishing economy based on fishing and farming as well as an overseas trade network that connected the area to Mesopotamia, the Indus Valley, Iran, and Oman (Crawford 1998, 51, 58). Circular stamp seals, pottery, stones used as weights, stone vessels, remains of buildings, graves, copper goblets and figurines, ivory boxes, and carved figures all testify to Dilmun's wealth and to its far-flung trading connections. In Oman, the Magan culture flourished through trading its copper to Mesopotamia and to the Indus Valley civilizations. Copper moving north to Mesopotamia from Magan most certainly passed through the trading center at Dilmun.

Magan's trade with Mesopotamia ceased about 2000 BC, when the Ur III dynasty there fell from power. Magan continued to trade with the Harappan civilization in the Indus Valley, but as the Harappans went into decline, so, too, did Magan. About 1800 BC, with the opening of a new trade route to Egypt through the Arabian Sea to the Gulf of Aden and into the Red Sea, where the pharaohs had dug a canal to link the Red Sea to the Nile, Dilmun, too, began to decline in importance. In addition, the development of land caravan routes across Arabia due to new technological developments (invention of the saddle, domestication of camels) drew off trade that originally had passed through the Gulf.

The Gulf continued to be a hotly contested area from this period forward. In 325 BC, Alexander the Great sent ships to explore the Arab side of the Gulf and established a few outposts there, but his successors lost control to the Persian Parthians (about 250 BC), who eventually controlled the region as far as Oman. Parthian conquest of the Gulf solidified two separate trading routes: the Greeks and Romans relied on the Red Sea route, while the Parthians relied on the Gulf route. The area was held under Persian control until the rise of Islam and the Muslim conquests of the peninsula after Muhammad's death in AD 632. Tribes in Bahrain and Oman are reported to have been among the early converts to the new religion. When the capital of the Islamic Abbasid Empire was moved to Baghdad from Damascus (in Syria), the Gulf again rose in importance for its trading networks. By the year 1000, Gulf traders were traveling to China, Indonesia, and Malaysia, taking their new religion with them (Metz 1994, 18). For a time, the Ismaili sect of Islam (see Chapter 2), represented by the Qarmatians (AD 899–1067), ruled from Bahrain, controlling the Gulf to Oman. Bahrain broke away in AD 1058, and orthodox Islam was restored as the religion of the land. In Oman, during roughly this same time, the Ibadi leaders established their control over the interior of the country, while the coasts were ruled by foreign powers, mainly Iranian leaders.

During the Middle Ages, the Gulf region's trade was controlled by Muslim leaders—either from Iraq or from Persia (what is now Iran). Control over East-West trade made Muslim merchants wealthy. Seeking to end Muslim control over valued resources like spices, silk, and other commodities, European sailors took to the seas in an effort to find a way to bypass the Muslim countries and seize direct control of the valuable trade with the East. The Portuguese were the first to succeed, and they used an alternate route, around the tip of Africa, to bring valued goods back to European port cities. They established trading bases in India, from which they eventually reached out to establish control over trade in the Arabian Gulf, capturing port cities in Oman and setting up forts and customhouses to exact tribute. Abbas I, Shah of Iran, invited the English and Dutch to help him root the Portuguese out of the Gulf, promising them favorable trading conditions in return. In 1622, the British succeeded in driving the Portuguese out of Hormuz, at the mouth of the Gulf; eventually, they became one of the major powers in the Gulf.

Taking advantage of Portuguese preoccupation with defending their interests from the Iranians and British, the Yarubid family of Omani imams was able to reconquer the coastal cities and reunite the interior and coast. Power struggles between the 1730s and 1750s allowed the Iranians to regain a foothold in Oman, but it was short-lived. In 1742, the al-Said family expelled the Iranians from the coast and became the rulers of a united Oman. They were able to expand Oman's control, eventually reaching as far as Bahrain and reestablishing Omani control over the island of Zanzibar and several other eastern African coastal cities.

During the eighteenth and nineteenth centuries, the Gulf region experienced considerable turmoil as Iranians and British, Ottoman Turks and Omanis all attempted to expand their control over the region. Into this volatile mix came the Wahhabi movement, which had its roots in the Arabian Peninsula. Muhammad ibn Abd al-Wahhab was a religious reformer who wanted to return Islam to its pure roots and to rid it of all foreign elements and practices. He joined forces in 1744 with Muhammad ibn Saud, ruler of a small town near Riyadh (now Saudi Arabia's capital). Under Ibn Saud, the Wahhabi forces conquered the peninsula. At various points in time, Ibn Saud attempted to expand his control into Oman, Kuwait, and Bahrain, but he was unsuccessful. Wahhabism, as a movement, did take root in Qatar, where the al-Thani family adopted it and used it to resist the attempts of the al-Khalifa to take control of Qatar. It also found root among the al-Qasimi of the UAE, who were engaged in trading along the coasts and to whom the antiforeign aspects of Wahhabism were especially compelling, given their efforts to resist the British takeover of the Gulf.

The British and the Qasimi confederacy inevitably clashed. As far as the Qawasim were concerned, the British were supporting their enemies and harming their livelihoods, which made British ships fair game for attacking and pillaging. For their part, English and Dutch traders of the time period labeled the Qawasim as pirates, and the coast came to be known as the Pirate Coast. The British decided that they had to destroy the Qasimi fleet once and for all and moved on Ras al-Khaimah in 1809, occupying the town and destroying most of the fleet anchored offshore. The Qawasim fought back, but the British were not through. In 1819–1820, they sent a large fleet from India to completely eradicate Qawasim ships in the Gulf. Ras al-Khaimah was again placed under siege, and this time, the British succeeded in destroying the entire Qasimi fleet. The al-Qasimi agreed to sign a truce, and one by one, all of the emirates along the coast signed agreements with the British, creating what came to be known as the Trucial system. The separate Gulf political units agreed not to attack the British on land or sea, and the British, for their part, indicated that they had no intentions of trying to politically control the area and would not interfere in local affairs. Bahrain signed a similar treaty with the British in 1861, and Kuwait did so in 1899, while Qatar's treaty was signed in 1916. The various local powers continued to fight with each other at sea for a few more years, but even those conflicts ended when they all signed the Perpetual Maritime Truce in 1853.

The British, in effect, became responsible for the defense of the Trucial states from outside enemies, and while Britain had said that it had no designs on the Gulf coast, in effect, Britain ruled the region by prohibiting Trucial states from making their own international agreements or hosting foreign delegations without British approval. The British helped local rulers fight off renewed attempts by the al-Saud family to take over the region as well as attempts by Ottomans and Iranians to establish control over Bahrain, and the Ottomans over Kuwait and Qatar. Gulf trade was further damaged by the opening of the Suez Canal and by the ending of the lucrative slave trade by 1900. What remained were the pearl beds, but the industry collapsed during the world depression in the 1930s, and by the time the depression was over, Japanese cultured pearls reduced the demand for and price of authentic pearls.

The rulers of Oman eventually also fell under British control. When a dispute arose over the succession to the Omani throne, the British seized the opportunity to give one brother control of Oman and the other control of Zanzibar, thereby severing Oman's eastern African territories and severely restricting the revenues of the sultan in Oman. Groups in the interior rose up against him, and he ended up calling the British in to protect him from his own people. Britain's dominance in the Gulf would last until 1971. With the discovery of oil in Bahrain in 1932, the British found themselves vying with the Americans for access to the Gulf's vast oil resources.

Before the discovery of oil, British control over the Gulf kept this area isolated from contact with other Arab countries and the rest of the world (except India; Zahlan 1989, 13). The British controlled movement in and out of the region. They required each ship to fly the flag of the state to which it belonged and issued travel documents, thus encouraging residents in the region to begin to see themselves as members of separate political entities. By dealing with local rulers, the British gave legitimacy and stability to their rule. By protecting them from outsiders, the British established the territorial identities of the modern states. This period of British control was largely responsible for the shape of the modern Gulf.

Foreign oil companies entered the region after World War I. Bahrain's oil concession was signed in 1930, Kuwait's in 1934, Qatar's in 1935, and Abu

Dhabi's in 1939. The entry of the oil companies brought out a new problem in the region—where, exactly, were the boundaries for each country (Zahlan 1989, 17)? Tribal law had never bothered with delineating what land belonged to which ruler—borders varied with ecological conditions. However, the oil companies wanted to know exactly where they were gaining the rights to search for oil. Thus a period of defining borders began. Kuwait's borders were fixed in 1922, at a British-led conference, where most of the land Kuwait was claiming was awarded to Saudi Arabia. Bahrain's borders were no issue (although Qatar has laid claim to some islands seen as part of Bahrain). Conflicts over borders for the other states continued over the next decades, and border disputes continue to flare up.

While oil exploration began in the region during the 1930s, this does not mean that oil wealth began to flow at that time. Exploration activities were interrupted by World War II, and commercially viable fields were not located immediately. Large deposits were found in Bahrain in the 1930s, but it was actually Kuwait's fields that were developed first, so that by 1953, Kuwait was the major oil producer in the Gulf. Qatar's fields came into production in the 1950s and Abu Dhabi's in 1962, while Dubai and Oman began exporting oil in the late 1960s. At the beginning, the oil companies were all foreign owned—British or American through British subsidiaries—and were able to set their own terms because the rulers in the Gulf were in a weak bargaining position. They had few other sources of revenue, given the destruction of the pearling industry in the 1930s. Over the years, though, each country was able to renegotiate the terms of the concessions. By the 1970s, as their wealth accumulated, the region's rulers were able to buy the majority of the shares of the subsidiaries working in their countries. By the 1990s, many of these companies were completely state owned (Metz 1994, 30).

Oil wealth revolutionized life in the Gulf states. Once concessions were signed, the Gulf region was no longer an isolated backwater. States in the region connected to other Arab nations, sending students to Lebanon, Egypt, and Iraq. Teachers from Lebanon, Palestine, and Egypt arrived in Kuwait and Bahrain to help in the process of establishing a national educational system. As wealth flowed into the region from oil, local rulers built schools, universities, hospitals and health care systems, roads, and power and desalination plants and created modern cities and towns.

By the 1960s, Great Britain was ready to end its treaty obligations in the Gulf. Kuwait declared its independence in 1961 and was immediately threatened with annexation by Iraq. Both the British and the newly formed Arab League sent troops to Kuwait to prevent Iraq from invading. A new Iraqi government formally renounced its claims on Kuwait in 1963. By the end of the decade, the British had decided to end their military involvement in the region. Qatar, Bahrain, and the various emirates entered talks about a possible nine-state federation. However, the ruler of Bahrain was not satisfied with the position of his country in the federation, and so he declared independence in August 1971; the government of Qatar quickly followed suit, declaring its independence in September 1971. The remaining emirates (with the exception of Ras al-Khaymah) decided to form a federation anyway (the UAE) and declared their independence in December 1971. Ras al-Khaymah, which pulled out of the negotiations due to lack of support for its claims to several islands and oil fields also claimed by Iran, quickly realized it could not function on its own and joined the new federation in February 1972.

Although Oman never gave up its independence, British involvement in the country had created resentment among the local population, who blamed the sultan for bringing in the foreigners. By 1958, the sultan had withdrawn to the city of Salalah in Dhofar and had cut the country off from the rest of the world. He discouraged any political reform or economic development. At the same time, Western companies were clamoring to look for oil in the interior of the country, and a Marxist rebellion (supported by the government of Yemen) was brewing in Dhofar. The Dhofar rebellion broke out in 1964; the sultan was forced to ask again for British assistance, which was then used against him as further proof of his unfitness to rule by the Dhofari rebels. The situation came to a climax in 1970, when the sultan was overthrown in a coup and replaced by his son Qaboos ibn Said. Qaboos moved to put down the rebellion in Dhofar using Arab assistance. He appealed to regional leaders to send forces and was able to end the rebellion by 1982, when he established diplomatic ties with southern Yemen and the government there stopped supporting the rebels. Sultan Qaboos removed the restrictions on development and moved to bring Oman into the modern world economy.

Overall, the region has remained relatively stable in recent years. Bahrain witnessed periodic outbreaks of violence throughout the 1980s and 1990s by its Shiite majority. The unrest stemmed from Shiite allegations of discrimination and mistreatment at the hands of the Sunni rulers. Their complaints centered on high rates of unemployment and demands for greater democracy in the country. The government accused Iran of being behind the unrest and responded strongly by imprisoning or exiling political activists.

Since the American invasion of Iraq in 2003, the outbreak of sectarian violence there between Sunnis and Shiites has threatened to spill over into the countries of the Gulf. Bahrain has continued to experience outbreaks of violence by its poor Shiite majority, with the most recent government crackdown occurring in April 2008. In Kuwait, Sunni bookstores were attacked in January 2008 by unknown (assumed to be Shiite) attackers, while in March 2008, there were several Shiite demonstrations in the capital of Kuwait City (although these were clearly not antiregime demonstrations). The UAE has been rocked by strikes and labor unrest, beginning in 2006 and continuing into the present, as foreign workers protest over inflation and unpaid wages. Here, too, the state has responded by threatening arrests and deportations, if workers did not direct their grievances through the appropriate official channels.

Oman and Qatar have deviated from other countries in the Arab world by preserving close ties with Iran as well as by establishing relationships with Israel. The Qataris and Iranians signed an agreement in 1991 for Iran to supply Qatar with freshwater via an undersea pipeline. In 1995, Qatar struck an agreement with Israel to supply Tel Aviv with natural gas (through a third party). In 1993, Sultan Qaboos of Oman was the first Gulf leader to host a representative of Israel in his country, when then prime minister Yitzchak Rabin visited Oman. Although the Israelis have attempted to establish low-level diplomatic relations with Bahrain and the UAE, so far, those efforts have not been successful. A great deal of popular opposition remains to such ties among the elected officials and citizens of the two countries. In Bahrain, a parliamentary committee called on the foreign minister to reopen the so-called Israeli Boycott Office, which was closed in 2005, when Bahrain signed a free trade agreement with the United States.

NOTES

1. The largest Israeli shipping firm, Zim, supported DPW acquiring these leases, writing in their letter of support that they had never had any security concerns about ports DPW managed and that they were proud to be associated with the company.

2. The Baluch are a tribal group whose territory is split between Iran, Pakistan, and Afghanistan. Baluch people began migrating to Oman over two hundred years before the 1900s.

3 Slavery was not formally abolished in Oman until 1970.

4. Central Intelligence Agency, *The 2008 World Factbook*, https://www.cia.gov/library/publications/the-world-factbook/.

5. Information about Healthcare City can be found at http://www.dhcc.ae/EN/Pages/Default.aspx; Media and Internet City at http://www.dubaiinternetcity.com/; the Palm at http://www.thepalm.ae/; Dubailand at http://www.dubailand.ae/.

2

Religion and Worldview

WHILE ISLAM IS the dominant religion in the Arab Gulf states, religious life there is much more varied than a casual observer might expect due to the role the region has played in commerce and transcontinental trade. Religious life is as rich as cultural life; you can find all the major variants of Islam, different forms of Christianity (Catholics and Protestants), Hinduism, and even small pockets of Buddhists and Jews. While the vast majority of the residents of the five countries are indeed Muslims (see Table 2.1), Christians, Hindus, and others account for between 4 percent and 17 percent of the population, found mainly within the populations of foreign workers living in each country.

In Bahrain, the ruling class of the al-Khalifa and their allies are Sunni Muslims, while the native farmers, fisherfolk, and divers on the island are Shia Muslim. In Qatar, most of the population are Sunni Muslims who adhere to the same strict Wahhabi interpretation of Islam as the Saudis, although in Qatar, unlike in Saudi Arabia, alcohol is available and women are allowed to drive automobiles. Most Omanis belong to the Ibadi sect of Islam, which traces its roots to the Kharajite rebellion against Ali ibn Abu Talib, fourth caliph. Immigrants from India in all the countries make up both those individuals following Hindu religious traditions and those following Christian traditions, particularly Pentecostal Christian and Catholic churches. The Catholic Church is also very popular, with large Filippino and Keralite (Indians from the state of Kerala) congregations.

Table 2.1
Religious Makeup of the Arab Gulf States (as of 2006), Including Indigenous Population (Mainly Muslims) and Expatriates (Other Religions)

Country	Muslims	Christians	Hindus	Others
Bahrain	83% Shia: 58% Sunni: 25%	10%	6%	
Kuwait	85% Shia: 30% Sunni: 45% Other: 10%	15% (includes Hindus)	15% (includes Christians)	
Oman	87.4% Ibadi: 75% Shia and Sunni: remainder	4.9%	5.7%	2.0% (includes 0.8% Buddhists)
Qatar	82.7% Shia: 14% Sunni: 68.7%	10.4%	2.5%	4.4%
United Arab Emirates	96% Shia: 16% Sunni: 80%	4% (includes Hindus)	4% (includes Christians)	

Source: Colbert Held, *Middle East Patterns*, 2006: 433–483.

ISLAM

Islam came to the Arab Gulf states very early. According to traditional accounts, Muhammad sent an emissary to Oman, then under Iranian control, to seek the conversion of its inhabitants. The Arab inhabitants of Oman, many of whom were Christian, embraced the new faith, but the Iranian garrison, which was Zoroastrian, did not. The new faith so inspired the Arab inhabitants that they were able to expel the Iranian garrison from their country. The Bani Abd al-Qais tribe that controlled Bahrain also converted to Islam early on. When Baghdad became the center of the Muslim Empire after AD 750, the Arab Gulf region prospered due to its trade with Iraq, and its merchants traveled as far away as China, taking their Islamic faith with them as they traded.

History

Islam had its birth in the Arabian Peninsula, in the city of Mecca. Mecca was a major trade center on the prosperous caravan route that ran along the western coast of Arabia, from Yemen to the Mediterranean. It attracted people also because of its local shrine, the Kaaba, a sanctuary built around the Black Stone of Mecca, which many different tribes held sacred and used as a place for the swearing of oaths. After worshipping at the Kaaba, tribesmen would later conduct their business in Mecca's markets (the *suqs*), where they could find goods from the Persians and the Byzantines. The wealth generated in that trade ended up concentrated in the hands of only a few people, however. As those individuals grew wealthy, they also began to neglect traditional tribal obligations to aid those less fortunate.

The Prophet Muhammad's own life circumstances must have made him acutely aware of the tensions that were beginning to surface in Meccan society. He was born into the Quraysh tribe around AD 570. His father died before he was born, his mother when he was six years old. The Prophet remained with members of his father's family to be raised and was cared for first by his grandfather, Abd al-Muttalib. When Muhammad was age eight, his grandfather died, and he went to live with his paternal uncle, Abu Talib, a wealthy merchant and head of the prestigious Bani Hashim clan. He worked for his uncle and traveled with his caravans on trading expeditions. During the course of these travels, he acquired a reputation as a skillful mediator of disputes. About 595, he was in charge of a caravan owned by a wealthy widow, Khadijah. She was so impressed with him that she married him; he was 25, she was 40. Khadijah bore him two sons (who died young) and four daughters.

Beginning in 610, the Prophet Muhammad began to receive revelations while spending the night thinking in a hill cave near Mecca. He was unsure about the visions at first but soon became convinced that he was receiving messages from God that should be shared with others. He gathered mainly young men from some of the mightiest Meccan families around him. He began to preach publicly in 613, facing little opposition. As he became more critical of the lifestyles of the wealthy merchants after 615, however, opposition to his teaching began to increase. Other clans also used opposing him as an opportunity to boycott his particular clan, without openly challenging their authority and power. When both his wife, Khadijah, and his uncle Abu Talib died in 619, the new leader of the clan withdrew its protection from the Prophet, forcing him to leave Mecca for a brief time, until he secured protection from another clan. The Prophet Muhammad and his followers continued to be harassed; his opponents even hatched a plot to assassinate him. Warned of the plot, he fled to Medina in 622 with his followers (an event that Muslims celebrate as the *hijrah*, the severing of kinship-ties).

In Medina, the Prophet Muhammad established the *umma*, the commonwealth of Muslims. Over the next eight years, he built his community, as he led his allies in attacks on Meccan caravans. Each successful attack attracted more followers. He also made a series of strategic marriage alliances, further strengthening his position there. As his fame grew, the status of Mecca's leaders fell. By 630, he was able to dictate the terms for his return to Mecca to the city's leaders. On returning, he took over control of the Kaaba and threw out the idols housed there. At this point, the terms of membership in the *umma* changed. After this time, if a new tribe or group wanted to join the *umma*, they had to accept Islam as their religion as well. The Prophet moved quickly to solidify his control over all of Arabia. By his death in 632, the peninsula was united, and Muslims were poised to expand outward. The Prophet died leaving his followers in limbo. He had no son who could succeed him, and he had not appointed a successor. Thus, at the moment of his death, the stage was set for the first split in Islam as different groups supported different individuals to take control of the faithful.

Some of the Prophet's followers believed that the right to rule should remain within the Prophet's family, based on the principle of patrilineal descent (inheriting through the male line) that traditionally was followed in Arabian society. They favored Ali, as the male relative who was most closely linked to the Prophet as his nephew and son-in-law. Others in the community favored selecting the next leader by means of consensus, and they prevailed, choosing the Prophet's trusted friend Abu Bakr, who became the first *khalifah*, or caliph (literally, "successor") and ruled until his death in 634. The principle of election continued, and Ali was passed over two additional times, as first Umar and then Uthman were named *khalifah*. The rule of each ended in assassination—Umar in 644 and Uthman in 656. With Uthman's death, Ali was finally elected *khalifah*, but political tensions had increased to the point that civil war broke out. Ali faced the forces of Uthman's relative Muawiyah and Muhammad's wife Aisha at the Battle of the Camel, but the outcome was ambiguous. When Ali agreed to arbitration, a section of his own followers rejected him in anger at his decision and broke off (the Kharijites, literally "those who go out"). Ali himself fell victim to assassination by a Kharijite in 661, and Muawiyah became ruler.

Muawiyah knew that Ali's sons and the Prophet's grandsons Hasan and Husayn would be strong candidates to lead the Muslims after he died. He wanted rule to remain in his family and so took steps to ensure that Ali's sons would never inherit. He poisoned Hasan, who died in 669. While still alive and powerful, he named his son Yazid as his successor. When he died in 680, Yazid was proclaimed caliph. However, many Muslims were upset with Umayyad rule and urged Husayn to revolt against Yazid. Their forces met at the Battle of Karbala in 680, where Husayn and his small band of seventy-two followers were defeated and slaughtered.

Husayn's death precipitated the split between what became known as the Sunni (*al-sunnah*, "the way of the Prophet") and Shia (*shiat Ali*, "partisans of Ali") sects of Islam. The Shia, as the minority, withdrew to Iran and Iraq, where they consolidated their power. Over time, as different sons of deceased Shia rulers were backed by different groups of followers, additional splits developed and new sects arose: Imamis ("Twelvers"), Ismailis ("Seveners"), and Zaydis ("Fivers"). The Ibadis, concentrated in Oman, split from both Sunni and Shia Islam; they see themselves as being the most faithful to the original Islam of the Prophet. Two additional sects that separated from the Ismaili tradition—the Alawis and the Druze—are viewed by mainstream Muslims as heretics.

Central Beliefs

The most important belief for Muslims is the oneness of God, a strict monotheism that is preached in the Quran, the set of revelations made to the Prophet Muhammad. Muslims demonstrate their submission to God's will through fulfilling obligations, known as the five pillars of Islam: *shahada*, the profession of faith; *salat*, daily prayers; *zakat*, almsgiving; *sawm*, fasting; and *hajj*, the pilgrimage to the holy city of Mecca.

The *shahada* proclaims that there is no god but God and Muhammad is his messenger. When the *shahada* is spoken in the presence of a religious official who vouches that the recital was sincere, the speaker has formally converted to Islam. Muslims pray five times a day, at dawn (*fajr*), midday (*dhuhr*), midafternoon (*asr*), sunset (*maghrib*), and nightfall (*isha'a*). The muezzin, a member of the community, calls Muslims to prayer by chanting aloud from a raised place (often the tower, or minaret, of the mosque). To pray, Muslims first ritually wash their hands, feet, and head (*wudu*). When water is not available, the ritual cleansing may be done with sand, as occurs in southern Qatar among the Bedouin who dwell there.

Once they have washed, Muslims face the direction of Mecca and go through the set movements of the prayers. They begin reciting the prayer while standing, and move through a series of proscribed positions, including bowing at the waist with hands on the knees, kneeling and prostrating so that only the forehead and the nose touch the earth, and sitting back on the heels before beginning the cycle again. The most important prayers are those that occur midday on Fridays at the mosque, where the congregants face the mihrab, a niche that indicates the direction of Mecca. After the prayers, the leading religious official in attendance delivers a sermon (*khutba*) that often refers to contemporary topics that affect the community. These sermons have often been used as vehicles for political announcements and even calls for revolt.

The *zakat* was an obligatory tax levied on food grains, cattle, and cash after one year's possession, with the amount of the tax varying according to different categories. The state collected the tax to support the poor, although it could also be used to ransom Muslim war captives, for education or health, or to redeem debts. With the breakup of the Ottoman Empire, the last Islamic empire, the *zakat* became a voluntary charitable donation. Many Muslims continue to practice the *zakat* by looking after their less fortunate family members, friends, or neighbors in times of need. In most of the Gulf states, payment of *zakat* remains voluntary, although there have been discussions in Bahrain about making the payments obligatory, and the United Arab Emirates (UAE) has moved to require all local Islamic banks and companies to pay 2.5 percent of their net operating capital to the Zakat Fund beginning in 2009. In Bahrain, the UAE, and Qatar, there are *zakat* funds set up, and individuals can even make online payments of the tax.[1] In Oman and Kuwait, payment of the tax is under the auspices of the Ministry of Religious Affairs and Endowments.

The fourth pillar, fasting (*sawm*), occurs during the month of Ramadan (the ninth month of the lunar calendar). From dawn to sunset, Muslims do not eat, drink, or smoke; only children under the age of puberty do not fast. Pregnant women, the sick, military personnel on active duty, and travelers are exempt from the fast but are expected to make up the missed days later. Once the sun goes down, the fast is ended for the day, and people can eat. This is why nights during Ramadan are festive occasions, with much visiting and exchange of hospitality.

The final pillar is the annual pilgrimage (*hajj*) to Mecca, which every Muslim should do once in his or her lifetime if he or she is able to afford to do it. During the twelfth lunar month, pilgrims from all over the world gather in Mecca to perform the complex ritual, which involves circumambulating the Kaaba seven times. While on pilgrimage, Muslims dress in two seamless white garments and refrain from sexual intercourse and from cutting their hair or nails, among other requirements. Because of their wealth and ease of access to Saudi Arabia, it is not uncommon to find pilgrims from the Gulf states who are making their fourth or fifth *hajj*.

Although usually not considered as one of the pillars of the faith, another important religious duty for Muslims is the concept of jihad, or struggle. Western commentators often focus on jihad as armed struggle or religious warfare on the behalf of Islam. However, within Islam, jihad more commonly refers to the struggle that occurs within the individual. This struggle involves improving one's self or one's society—resisting evil, pursuing what is just and good, and bringing about change to better one's society. Religious scholars quote a Hadith (saying of the Prophet) in which Muhammad speaks to the warriors to tell them that now that they have returned from the lesser jihad of fighting non-Muslims, they must now fight the greater jihad against their own natures. Muhammad viewed this internal struggle as the key one—the struggle to speak the truth and do right.

Sacred Days

The *ids* are the two most important holidays. Id al-Fitr, at the end of Ramadan, lasts for three days. People celebrate by buying new clothes, gift giving, entertaining, and visiting family graves at cemeteries. Id al-Adha, the last day of the pilgrimage, is celebrated by Muslims throughout the world by offering sacrifice (a sheep, goat, camel, or cow) in remembrance of Abraham's willingness to sacrifice his son Ishmael. The resulting meat is divided among pilgrims, the poor, and friends and neighbors. Both *ids* are times for attending the mosque and visiting and feasting with friends and family. Muhammad's birthday, Mawlid al-Nabi, is celebrated as a national holiday in some Gulf states. Special sermons in the mosques highlight the key events of the Prophet's life, while celebrations in homes feature reciting from the Quran and singing religious hymns. There is debate within the region as to whether this holiday should be celebrated, with some factions insisting it is forbidden since it was added after the death of Muhammad and so breaks with the idea that the complete form of Islam is that which was revealed to the Prophet before his death. Lailat al-Miraj commemorates the Prophet Muhammad ascending to heaven following his night journey from Mecca to Jerusalem. Lailat al-Qadr (Night of Power) celebrates the first revelation of the Quran. The first of Muharram, New Year's Day, marks the flight of Muhammad from Mecca to Medina. The tenth of Muharram, Ashura, is celebrated by Shia Muslims to commemorate the martyrdom of Husayn, the Prophet's grandson.

Shia, Ibadi, and Wahhabi Islam

What sets Shia Islam apart from Sunni Islam is a sixth pillar of the faith: the Shia belief in the imam, a leader who alone knows the hidden and true meaning of the Quran. Imams were descended from the Prophet Muhammad. With the disappearance of the twelfth imam in the ninth century, Shiite belief focused on the imam as a leader who is now hidden and who will return at the end of time to bring justice to the world. *Mujtahids* (Shiite religious leaders) are guided by the imam as they make doctrine and interpret law. They offer themselves as moral guides to their followers. In this way, the Shiite clergy are more hierarchical and centralized than their Sunni counterparts. Shia Islam itself fragmented into further sects, such as the Zaidi, Ibadi, Ismaili, Alawi,

and Druze, as different factions recognized different leaders as the true successors to the imamate. Some of the offshoots, such as the Druze, are actually no
longer viewed as Muslims because they have incorporated elements of other
belief systems into their religion.

Because of Sunni persecution, Shia Islam has come to emphasize elements
of suffering, martyrdom, and opposition to established power (particularly
when that power is seen as corrupt). Like Sunnis, Shiite Muslims practice the
five pillars of the faith; there are slight differences in daily practices, with a
different call to prayer, different ways of performing the ritual washing and
prostrations during prayer, and their practice of praying three times a day,
instead of five. There are also differences in which Hadiths they recognize.

Ibadi Islam developed out of the Khariji sects, who broke with the fourth
caliph, Ali, when he agreed to hold discussions with his main rival for the
leadership of the Islamic community. The Kharijis believed that in compro-
mising, Ali had been rendered unworthy of becoming the leader of Islam.
The sect takes its name from Abdullah bin Ibad al-Murri al-Tamimi, who
lived during the late seventh century. Abdullah's successor, Jabir ibn Zaid
al-Azdi, collected the Ibadi Hadith and doctrine and moved his followers from Iraq to Oman, where Ibadism took root. A hereditary imamate
developed in Oman in the mid-eighth to late ninth centuries, and that
imamate, although suppressed at times, survived in Oman well into the twentieth century.

Ibadi beliefs place great stress on clear distinctions between moral and
immoral leadership. It is a conservative movement that reads the Quran
literally. While strict on their own members, the sect displays tolerance to
outsiders. Ibadis believe that the imam should be chosen by the elders of the
community on the basis of his knowledge and piety and that if he became an
unjust ruler, the community had the obligation to depose him. The last true
imam was Ahmad ibn Said (ruled AD 1754–1783), who united the entirety of
Oman under his rule. His successors first used the title *sayyid*, shifting later to
sultan.

Wahhabi Islam represents a reformist movement within Sunni Islam influenced by the writings of the eighteenth-century scholar Muhammad ibn Abd
al-Wahhab. Abd al-Wahhab called for Muslims to return to the foundations of
their faith and to follow Islam as it was practiced during the first three generations. In preaching a more puritanical form of Islam, he rejected practices like
praying to saints and tomb and shrine visitation, which he saw as holdovers of
pre-Islamic practices. He preached a return to a strict form of Islam as the an-
tidote to the moral decline that he saw around him in the Arabian Peninsula.
It was a powerful message, with important consequences for the region. Abd
al-Wahhab, in making an alliance with the Ibn Saud family in the Arabian

Peninsula, put his holy warriors, the *ikhwan*, under the control of Ibn Saud, as he sought to unite the Arabian Peninsula under his control. Just as early Islamic armies swept to victory as they moved out of the Arabian Peninsula, Ibn Saud's forces captured the Muslim sacred sites of Mecca and Medina and much of the Arabian Peninsula, controlling the territory that became the modern country of Saudi Arabia. In Qatar, Wahhabi Islam is the dominant sect, although Qataris are not as strict in their observance as are Saudis.

Islam and the Life Cycle

Birth rites in Islam are recommended (*sunna*), rather than obligatory. Children born to Muslim parents are Muslim, and therefore there is no need of a ceremony to make them Muslim. When the birth is announced to the father, celebrations and gift giving occur. Women trill for joy. In the UAE, after mother and child are cleaned, the call for prayer is spoken into the baby's right ear. A male child receives a larger, grander celebration than a female child. Special foods may be cooked for the mother and child. One birth rite calls for the parent or a pious person to chew a bit of date until soft and place it in the mouth of the newborn (the *tahnik*).

On the seventh day, an additional rite may be carried out, a ritual substitution (*aqiqah*). The child's head is shaved, and money the weight of the hair is distributed to the poor. The naming ceremony takes place at this time as well. Parents give children names of family members, saints, or hoped-for characteristics. If a family has previously lost boys, they might give a new son the name of a girl to mislead evil powers and ensure his life. The new baby and the mother are believed to be vulnerable to evil spirits at this time, and so both are often protected by specially prepared amulets. The mother may also keep a copy of the Quran next to her bed.

Traditionally, in the UAE, when a baby was born, the midwife would cut the umbilical cord and tie it in three knots. She would then dispose of the afterbirth quickly and clean the mother and child with hot water, salt, and herbs. People in the UAE believed that individuals remain spiritually and physically linked to their cords and afterbirth. Therefore, it was important that they be properly disposed of and carefully buried. Families who wanted their child to be pious might bury the cord next to a mosque; if they wanted them to be a good student, they'd bury it beside a school. Nowadays, women give birth in hospitals and private clinics, so the cord and afterbirth are disposed of by the hospital officials, and the old traditions have died (Hurreiz 2002).

The next rite of passage is circumcision (*khitan*). It is a popular practice, rather than a religious one, and as such varies from region to region. Circumcision traditionally occurs at an age when the child is aware and will remember it (between two and twelve), although in modern times, some parents are having it performed at birth or in the first few days after birth. The traditional rituals are commonly held during the month of the Prophet's birthday and are performed by the barber. Given the wealth now present in the Arab Gulf states, 85 percent of circumcisions there are now performed by doctors or medical technicians, and only 15 percent are done by traditional practitioners (Rizvi et al. 1999). Before the operation, the boy is dressed in special clothes and paraded through the neighborhood or village; a long festive meal and gift giving may occur either before or after the ceremony. Once he is circumcised, a young boy enters the world of men.

There is debate about whether young girls are still circumcised in the Arab Gulf states. One estimate is that about 85 percent of families in the UAE either still observe the practice or have observed it until recently (Hurreiz 2002). It was said that once a girl was circumcised, she became more shy and would not go out of the house, that she was pure and ready for marriage, that she was more mature, and that she would no longer act like males. Anthropologist Unni Wikan (1982, 44) mentions a group of smiths, the Zatut of Sohar, who perform "circumcision of boys and girls"; Liesal Graz (1982, 138) mentions that it is not common and that when it occurs, it is mainly among people of African origin or in Dhofar; and a United Nations Children's Fund report mentions the practice occurring in Oman as well. Female circumcision is not an Islamic practice but most likely a holdover from pre-Islamic practices.

Muslim death rites are simple. Normally, a dead person is to be buried on the day of death. First, the corpse is bathed (*ghusl*) by persons of the same gender to remove any impurities. In Kuwait, the body is perfumed with rose oil, aloe, wood, and camphor. The corpse is then wrapped in a white shroud composed of three pieces for a man and five pieces for a woman to cover it completely. The funeral prayer for the dead is performed in the mosque. The corpse is carried to the graveyard for burial by a procession of relatives, friends, and other community members. The corpse is placed in the grave with its face turned toward Mecca and the Kaaba. Each person in attendance throws three handfuls of earth in the grave. On the third day after the burial, relatives visit the grave and recite passages from the Quran. The bereaved family is paid visits of condolence before and after the burial.

The Legal System (Sharia)

The body of laws that govern all aspects of a Muslim's life is known as the Sharia. Muslims hold the Quran to be the literal word of God. As such, it cannot be translated into any other language and retain its validity. In addition to the Quran, Muslims draw on the collected sayings of the Prophet Muhammad, known as the Hadith. The Hadith provide anecdotes about the proper way to live one's life (*sunna*). The Quran and the Hadith are the major sources for Islamic law. In the eighth century, scholars introduced the concept of *ijma*, or consensus. For those elements of the Quran or Hadith for which consensus had been reached, interpretation was closed and further questioning was prohibited. Over the years, to find solutions to new problems, a body of opinions based on analogy (*qiyas*) has been built up as Islamic judges interpreted the Quran and Hadith to deal with matters introduced due to changes in lifestyles.

Different schools of Islamic law developed in different parts of the Muslim world. All of them accord the Quran and Hadith importance. *Hanafi* law developed in Iraq under the Abbasids and is found primarily in areas of former Ottoman rule; it has the most followers. It is a relatively liberal law code that emphasizes the use of reason in making decisions. Shafii law is also more liberal, relying on consensus and the decisions of the judges. Maliki law, followed by Muslims mainly in northern and western Africa, adds the practice of the people of Medina as a potential source for making legal rulings. Hanbali law, found mainly in Saudi Arabia, draws its rulings from the Quran and the best of the Hadith; individual interpretation should be used only if absolutely necessary. Shiites follow Jaafari law, which regards *ijtihad* (independent reasoning) as a significant resource in legal analysis, or Akhbari law, which takes a more restrictive view of *ijtihad*. The Ibadis have their own form of Sharia. In the Arab Gulf states, one can find adherents of Maliki, Shafii, Hanbali, Ibadi, Jaafari, and Akhbari schools in different countries.

CHRISTIANITY

According to tradition, Christianity was introduced to the Arabian Peninsula by the Apostle Bartholomew. There was a Christian bishopric in the Bahrain Islands by the mid-third century, and Arab bishops were mentioned as attending the Council of Nicea, held in AD 325 (Strickert 2000, 68). However, as Islam spread in the region, Christianity faded, and there are no records about any Christian presence in the region for more than a millennium. As Europeans made contact in the Gulf region, Christianity was reintroduced. The Roman Catholic vicariate was established in 1889, while Protestant missionaries were also active in the region at about the same time period. While missionary activity was occurring, conversions were few, possibly no more than one thousand indigenous Christians in the whole Arabian Peninsula (Strickert 2000, 71). The large numbers of Christians to be found in the Gulf today are due to the presence of foreign workers from Palestine, Jordan, Lebanon, Syria, Egypt, India, and the Philippines and other Asian countries. These workers account for the presence of Greek Orthodox, Greek Catholic, Roman Catholic, Syrian Orthodox, Anglican, and evangelical congregations there. The Arab Gulf states allow freedom of worship but prohibit non-Muslim religious groups from proselytizing, attempting to convert Muslims to their faith. In addition, non-Muslim places of worship are not allowed to display crosses or any other visible signs of their faith on their buildings.

The first church built in Bahrain was constructed in 1906 by American Anglicans. The first Roman Catholic church in the region was built in Bahrain in 1939. Roman Catholics in the Gulf can now worship at three churches in Kuwait, four in Oman, and seven in the UAE. With the construction of a church in Qatar on land donated by the emir, which opened in 2008, religious pluralism in the region has been formally recognized by all governments of the Arab Gulf states. There are Roman Catholic schools in Bahrain and the UAE, which are attended by Muslim as well as Roman Catholic students. The Muslim students at the schools receive their religious instruction in Islam, in keeping with the no-proselytizing rules of the government. Qatar will allow four more churches to be built there to serve the other Christian groups in the country. There are Anglican churches in the UAE, Kuwait, and Oman, an Indian Orthodox church in Abu Dhabi, and Baptist and various Pentecostal congregations who meet in schools, homes, and other rented facilities throughout the emirates. This is the pattern across the five countries: Roman Catholic and Protestant congregations are allowed to hold services in every country, as long as they do not try to convert Muslims and do not bring public attention to their faith practices. This openness to other religions often surprises outsiders, who expect the Arab Gulf countries to be as rigid as Saudi Arabia is in forcing non-Muslim religious observance into private.

HINDUISM

Most Hindus in the Gulf region are foreign workers from India, mainly men attracted to the region by the oil boom and women who enter domestic service as maids, cooks, and governesses. However, Oman had a significant indigenous Hindu population that dated to immigrant merchants who settled in Muscat in 1507 from the Sindh region of the Indian subcontinent. In the early nineteenth century, the Hindu presence in Oman numbered several thousands, but over the next decades, the community came under attack, and by the time Oman became independent, only a few dozen Hindus remained. Today, it is estimated that there are about three hundred thousand Hindus in Oman, largely due to recent labor migrations there. Much of daily Hindu worship takes place within the home, but Hindu temples have been built in Bahrain, Oman, and the UAE, where larger ceremonial gatherings are held for religious festivals.

Hinduism is the third largest religion in the world (after Christianity and Islam) and is regarded by most as the oldest organized religion. There are many different forms of Hinduism, but most recognize a single deity, with different gods and goddesses representing aspects or variations of that supreme deity. Brahman, the supreme deity, is seen as representing reality and the universe while, at the same time, transcending it. Brahman is envisioned as one deity with three forms: Brahma the Creator, Vishnu (Krishna) the Preserver, and Shiva the Destroyer. Hindus believe in the transmigration of souls—that after death, an individual's soul is reborn into another body. You earn karma throughout your life based on your good and bad deeds. At death, your accumulated balance of karma determines how your soul will be reborn in the next life. The more good deeds one does, the more likely one is to be born at a higher level in the next life.

Hindus are divided into those who are in the world and those who have renounced the world. For Hindus who remain in the world, their goal in life is to lead a righteous life (*dharma*), enjoy material prosperity (*artha*), and find pleasure in living (*kama*). Those who have renounced the world seek to be liberated from the continuing cycle of rebirth and to achieve enlightenment (*moksa*). Hinduism includes among its practices meditation (such as yoga), daily devotional prayers, public rituals, and *puja* (offerings given to a god such as flowers, food, or clothing). Observant Hindus have a shrine in their homes to their family gods. On a normal day, an observant Hindu would begin his or her day by washing, then praying to the family deity and spending some time reading from the scriptures and meditating. A portion of one's breakfast might be offered to the family deity before eating it. In the evening, the entire family gathers for family prayers, followed by dinner and additional praying to the family deity before going to bed. Hindus are also expected to participate in religious festivals, such as Diwali (the Festival of Lights) and Holi (the Festival of Colors), and to go on pilgrimage to sacred sites.

A recurring theme in Hinduism is the opposition of pollution and purity. Hindus are called on to avoid pollution and strive for purity. Purification requires using water to cleanse oneself and avoiding impure things: eating flesh, associating with dead things, and body fluids. This attention to levels of purity is at the heart of the caste system as it developed in India. Members of the highest castes were individuals who were seen as the most pure in their actions and lifestyle. Individuals who came into contact with dead things and bodily secretions through their work activities were viewed as untouchables, literally outside the boundaries of the caste system. The caste system dictated the entire circumstances of one's life, from the clothes one wore and the foods eaten to one's occupation and marriage partner. It was a closed system—one's only hope for upward movement was to lead a righteous life and to be reborn into a higher caste. Today, the caste system has been outlawed by the Indian government, but Hindus continue to recognize caste status informally, and many marriages are still arranged within caste boundaries.

RELIGION AND POLITICS

Within Islam, religion and politics have always been intertwined since Muhammad established the first *umma*, or community of believers. Muslim tradition is very clear about how Muslims should be governed: Muslim governments are expected to provide just and moral leadership through consulting with their citizens. Islam provides the way to lead life—whether for an individual or for a state. Secularism, the belief that religion and government should be separated, was an idea that developed in the West out of uniquely Western historical experiences of religious disagreement and strife. It was introduced to the Middle East when Europeans colonized that region in the eighteenth and nineteenth centuries. While some Middle Eastern states declared themselves to be secular on independence, the states of the Arab Gulf region established themselves as Islamic states, recognizing the Sharia as their guiding principle. Some scholars call the current surge in Islamic political activism worldwide "political Islam," but it is important to understand that Islam has always united politics with religion.

A key issue for the Arab Gulf states where religion and politics meet concerns the form of government. Sunni and Shiite Muslims, and secular and religious Muslims, struggle throughout the region over how their states should be governed. The Shiite government of Iran has been accused by other Arab countries with significant Shia populations of trying to export revolution to their states, as a means of realizing the goal of reestablishing Muslim dominance in the world. Tensions can surface in the Arab Gulf states about the quality and justice of the rulers, and rulers there must pay particular attention to their Islamic obligations to look after the welfare of their citizens. However, they also face complaints from their more secular citizens, who wish to see more democratic freedoms in these same countries. The success of these states in modernizing, without alienating their residents or producing significant forms of social inequality, is partly a function of the skills of their rulers in maintaining their legitimacy as good Muslim leaders and as good progressive leaders. Democratic reforms and progressive world views hold sway currently among the rulers of the five countries, but within an Islamic framework.

An excellent example of such a skilled leader is Sultan Qaboos bin Said bin Taimur al-Bu Saidi of Oman. He took control of Oman in 1970, forcing his father to abdicate. Under Sultan Said, Oman was one of the most isolated and backward regions of the Middle East. Sultan Qaboos was able to defeat a Marxist uprising, unite the country, and begin the process of modernizing Oman's infrastructure by building schools, roads, hospitals, and public housing as well as by revitalizing the economy by strategic investments there. He approved a basic constitution for Oman in 1996, allowed limited elections for a Majlis al-Shura (Consultative Council) in 1997, and in 2003, extended universal suffrage for the Majlis elections that October. Under his rule, Oman has prospered and has the lowest level of political or economic tension in the region (Held 2006, 179).

NOTE

1. See http://www.zakatfund.net/en/index.php for the UAE and http://www.zf.org.qa/english/index.htm for Qatar.

3

Literature and Media

GULF LITERATURE IS only now beginning to make its mark on the literary scene in the rest of the Arab world, much less the English-speaking world. Less well known Gulf writers are beginning to be included in Arabic anthologies of short stories from various Arab countries, giving their work a wider base of circulation (Ramsay 2006b, 252–253). Very few Gulf authors have been translated into English (Mohammad al-Murr of Dubai, with two English collections of short stories, is the notable exception).[1]

One issue that hampers writers in Arabic to an extent not seen for writers in other languages is the diglossia present in the Arabic-speaking world. Diglossia refers to the situation where two different languages are spoken within a society. One language is usually perceived as high prestige and may be used in government and media, while the other language is low prestige and represents the language of the street (also called the vernacular). The high-prestige form of the language is taught in the schools and is the mark of an educated person. Arabic is considered just such a language. It exists in a classical form (Fusha; also called modern standard) and in a variety of spoken regional dialects (which are often mutually unintelligible). Classical Arabic, the language of the Quran, was preserved as a sacred language because the Quran was seen as the literal word of God and thus the Quran could not be translated into other languages. Muslims all over the world memorize the Quran in classical Arabic. As the Arab Empire spread, however, Arabic mixed and mingled with a variety of other languages spoken in the conquered territories to create vernaculars, or different variants, of spoken Arabic.

For the writer, this creates problems. Gulf writers who use regional dialects in their stories' dialogues to give their writing more realism and meaning for their local audiences then face the difficulty of having to retranslate and, in effect, rewrite their works if they are to be read by an Arabic-speaking, non-Gulf audience. This helps to explain why Gulf literature is only now beginning to make its mark on the broader field of Arabic (and world) literature. Those Gulf writers who write in classical forms of the language run the risk of not being read by their own local audience, for whom classical Arabic may be difficult. As the publishing establishment in the Gulf world matures and expands, writers will have the necessary resources at their disposal to deal with these issues of diglossia.

In the Gulf at present, governments see production of distinct literatures as an important part of nation building as the literature helps to shape or create unique and distinctive national identities (as Kuwaitis, Omanis, Qataris, Bahrainis, or Emiratis). Therefore, the governments provide substantial support for writers through government foundations or associations. Writers also may receive support from private foundations and private literary magazines. Writers' unions in the various countries serve to bring accomplished and aspiring writers together for the purpose of advancing the craft of writing. One of the most important early outlets for writers were local newspapers and magazines, which would publish short stories or poetry. Unfortunately, some of the earliest literary works have not been preserved because archives were not necessarily well organized, and very early papers or magazines have been lost.

Folk Traditions

The earliest roots for literature in the region would have been in oral folk literature (folktales, poetry, proverbs, and riddles). Oral folktales are still very popular, although traditional storytelling sessions are being displaced by modern mass media and entertainment such as television, videos, and electronic games. One example of such a folktale from the United Arab Emirates (UAE), called a *kharrūfa*, represents an Arabic version of the Western Cinderella story (Hurreiz 2002, 74–75). In this version, known as "The Fisherman's Daughter," the father is a fisherman and is urged to remarry a kindly neighbor by his daughter. Once the new wife has daughters of her own, however, she begins to treat her stepdaughter unkindly. The stepdaughter is sent to clean and cut up fish every day. One fish is still alive and begs for mercy, offering to help her whenever she is in need, and the stepdaughter returns it to the sea. The fish feeds her when she is hungry and provides clothing for her to go to the sheikh's celebration, where his son falls in love with her. She flees from his attentions but leaves her golden shoes behind. The sheikh's son searches for her using the shoes, and when he comes to her house, her stepmother forces her to hide inside the oven. All is saved when the cock crows out that the girl is in the oven. The oven is searched, she is found, the shoes fit, and she marries the sheikh's son and lives in happiness.

Besides these folktales, another genre of oral story exists in the region—the legend (*sālfa*)—which is rooted in the past in a specific locality and which may combine past events with imaginative twists. Such tales teach important lessons about life and about tribal or community values and expectations for behavior. One such tale is that of the young man who tests the advice his dying father gave him. His father told him not to marry his sister to a stranger, not to entrust any woman with his secrets, and not to trust an illegitimate child. The young man goes on with his life and eventually marries one sister to a stranger and finds an abandoned, illegitimate child, whom he raises as his own. Both sister and child prosper, so he begins to doubt his father's advice. He tests it when he finds a sheep that belonged to the sheikh, which he hides away and cares for. He brings home meat and fat from the butcher, and his wife asks where they came from. He decides to tell her he has slaughtered the sheikh's sheep. She in turn divulges his secret to an old woman, who turns him in to the sheikh for a reward. When the man did not heed the sheikh's call to present himself, the abandoned child he had raised was the one who seized him and delivered him to the sheikh. He was fined ten camels. When he turned to the stranger who had married his sister, the man turned his back on him, providing only one sickly camel to help him pay the fine. The man received true help from the husbands of his other sisters, who had been married to their cousins. He took ten good camels to the sheikh, with his sheep, and explained he had wanted to test his father's advice. The relatives who came to his assistance were richly rewarded, while the fickle brother-in-law received only his sickly camel in return (Hurreiz 2002, 76–78).

Besides folktales, folk poetry, proverbs, and riddles are also important elements of local oral traditions. As with folktales, poetry and proverbs were important vehicles for transmitting social values, traditional customs, and folk knowledge. Poetry and proverbs are highly valued forms of expression within Arab culture. Proverbs such as "Hair falling from the mustache rests on the beard" (*alli yahit min al shārib taltaqīh al lihya*) remind the listeners that when misfortune falls on their relatives, it also affects them as well (Hurreiz 2002, 82). Riddles, expressed as general statements, instead of questions, were drawn from rural or nomadic life.

Poetry

Poetry is a well-defined literary form within the Arab world, and it has been said that it represents the true genius of the Arab people. Poets writing in the Gulf today have been influenced by modern developments and new forms that have come into Arabic poetry through contact with the West. As Arab poets encountered the work of T. S. Eliot after World War II, movements to incorporate free verse, prose poems, and social realism within Arabic poetry took root. Poetry in the vernacular, *al-nabati*, is popular with young poets, who have adapted more traditional forms and motifs to shorter poems intended to be sung. When in translation, it is difficult to see the differences between prose poems and free verse. However, in the original Arabic, one can see that a prose poem has neither rhyme nor metric structure, while free verse still incorporates free metrical structures and unconventional rhyme schemes. Free verse works to preserve the musicality that existed in classical Arabic poetry, with its named meters. Works by male and female poets from all Gulf countries can be found in English translation.

Ibrahim al-Urayyid (1908–), an early modern Bahraini poet, was born in India to a pearl merchant father and an Iraqi mother, who died while he was still an infant. He returned to Bahrain when he was twenty, where he studied Arabic. His first poems were written in Urdu and English, although he later excelled in Arabic as well. He was followed by 'Ali 'Abdallah Khalifa (1944–), who helped found the Union of Bahraini Writers; Abd al-Rahman Rafi' (1938–), who wrote folk and traditional formal poetry and free verse; and 'Ali al-Sharqawi (1948–), an experimental Gulf poet who also writes folk poetry, poetry, and plays for children. Well-known female poets include Hamda Khamees (1946–), Fawziyya al-Sindi, and Thurayya al-Urayyid, sixth daughter of well-known poet Ibrahim al-Urayyid.

One of the most well known Bahraini poets is Qassim Haddad (1948–). Haddad is self-educated. He served as director of culture and arts in the Ministry of Information and chaired the National Writer's Union. He has published over sixteen books of poetry and prose and writes literary criticism for Arab newspapers and magazines. Haddad is part of the free verse movement. His poetry deals with themes of freedom, progress, love, and revolution. His poems available in English translation include "The Feast of the Sea," "As They Say," "Answer," "Words from a Young Night," "The Friends There," "Body," "The Pearl," "The Children," "All of Them," and "Like the White."

Kuwaiti poets include Ahmad al-Mushari al-'Udwani (1923–), who completed an Islamic education at al-Azhar University in Egypt, and Khalifa al-Wugayyan (1941–), who studied Arabic literature in Cairo at 'Ain Shams University. A strong voice of social and political dissent in the region, al-'Udwani has held the position of director general of the National Council for Culture, Arts, and Literature. Al-Wugayyan has a reputation in Kuwait for his innovations in poetry. His poems in translation include "Letter to a Bedouin Informer" and "Elegy in Memory of Yusuf al-Babtain." Prominent female poets include Su'ad al-Mubarak al-Sabah (1942–), a member of the royal family of Kuwait, and Sa'adyya Mufarreh, who is arts editor of *al-Qabas* newspaper. Al-Sabah has been an active supporter of the arts as well as an active participant in pan-Arab organizations for freedom, human rights, and Arab unity. Her poems include "Mad Woman," "Free Harbor," "You Alone," "A Wild Cat," and "The Pit."

Sayf al-Rahabi (1956–) and Muhammad al-Harthi (1962–) represent two different strands of verse in Oman. Al-Rahabi is a prose poet, while al-Harthi has been writing surrealistic free verse since 1982. Other Omani poets include Sama' Isa (another surrealist) and Hilal al-Amiri (a modernist). Qatar's Ali Mirza Mahmud (1952–) is also a modernist and cofounded the Qatari Theatre Group, while Mubarak bin Saif al-Thani (1950–) works in the Ministry of Foreign Affairs and was awarded the poetry prize by the Spanish-Arab Institute for Culture and Art in 1985. Female poet Zakiyya Malallah (1959–) has seen her poetry translated into Spanish, Urdu, and Turkish. Her poems in English include "Little Tales" and "Women."

Two well-known female poets from the UAE are Dhabya Khamees (1958–) and Maysoun Saqr al-Qasimi (1958–). Khamees was educated in the United States, Egypt, and London. Her poetry expresses strong confidence in her identity as a woman. Khamees was kidnapped and imprisoned in 1987 for five months in Abu Dhabi as punishment for her writing, and her books were banned. She currently resides in Egypt and, since 1992, has worked for the Arab League. She has published three short story collections and numerous books of poetry, mainly in Cairo. Her poetry has been translated into English, Russian, German, Dutch, and Urdu. Al-Qasimi writes in a more experimental mode about the relationships between men and women. She, too, was educated in Cairo and has had her work published in numerous journals and anthologies in both the Arabic-speaking world and in translation. Two other female poets, Sarah Harib (1959–) and Ru'a Salim (1957–), write using pen names.

Prose

Prose—comprising short stories, novels, and novellas—is a modern introduction into the region, where it made its first appearance in the early 1900s. The earliest literature was found in Kuwait, possibly inspired by students returning to Kuwait from Egypt, where they had been sent on study missions and had been exposed to Western and modern Arabic literary forms. The first Kuwaiti short story, written by Khalid al-Faraj, was published in the Iraqi journal *al-Kuwait* in 1928. Short stories began to appear in Bahrain in the 1940s and 1950s and in the UAE and Qatar in the 1970s. Modern literature appears most recently in Oman, where a modern educational system was not constructed until after 1970, when Sultan Qaboos assumed power.

The establishment of modern educational systems has been essential to the development of literature throughout the countries of the Gulf. Once each country began to educate its citizens, within a few decades, modern literature began to appear.

Gulf literature developed in tandem with the economic, social, and political modernization of Gulf states. Thus it comes as no surprise that this literature largely documents, comments on, and satirizes the effects of the oil wealth and the modernization it brought on more traditional ways of life (Michalak-Pikulska 2004). Work after work illustrates the strains and contradictions as the traditional and modern collide. The role and status of women is highlighted in a number of works, and not just works by female authors. Many writers also comment on the social disruptions that oil has brought to the region. Poor people suddenly find themselves rich, but their newfound wealth does not necessarily bring happiness. Class distinctions within the society are more pronounced, and people forget their traditional obligations to look after those less fortunate than themselves. The influx of foreign workers creates new categories of residents in the countries of the region who do not share in the wealth that oil has brought.

Literary critics writing about Gulf literature recognize three distinct styles (Ramsay 2002–2003): realistic, magical realism, and modernist. Works that belong to the realist genre deal with the clash between modern, Western values and expectations and traditional Gulf culture. The works are often critical of the transformations taking place in their societies. Patriarchal culture is often the focus of works by women, who note the new freedoms available to women in the region (access to education, ability to work, luxurious lifestyles), while, at the same time, women remain bound by traditional notions of family honor and responsibility. In their stories, husbands cheat on wives, and women are held hostage in their homes, unable to use their new educations to bring about needed social change in their societies.

Magical realism, like its Latin American counterparts, draws on traditional folk imagery and beliefs—djinns, magic, the evil eye—but recycles it into modern, realistic settings, settings that could potentially be anywhere in the world. Gulf writers have a rich Arabic literary heritage to draw from in bringing the past into their stories, using themes reminiscent of *A Thousand and One Nights* and characters drawn from other traditional folktales known to residents of the region. In such works, humans turn into animals, djinns and humans marry, and characters find themselves transported in the blink of an eye to new realities.

The final modernist trend focuses more on how works should be written than on the subject matter (Ramsay 2002–2003, 374). Such writing draws its inspiration from the forms of Arabic poetry—the fixed stylistic forms, rich metaphorical language, and use of metaphor and simile. Some literary critics refer to this trend as the Arabic "very short" story due to the briefness and condensed style. Such pieces require their readers to fill in the gaps and insert the required meanings as they move from sentence to sentence in the piece. The writers make use of Arabic plays on words with multiple meanings, the correct one of which the reader must discern for himself or herself. These pieces are thus particularly difficult to translate into other languages.

English speakers who wish to read Gulf literature are limited to works from Kuwait and the UAE. Among writers in the UAE, Mohammad al-Murr, born in Dubai in 1955, is the only one who has published two collections of his short stories in English: *Dubai Tales* and *The Wink of the Mona Lisa*. Al-Murr studied at Syracuse University in the United States and worked as a journalist in the UAE. He has published a total of eleven collections of short stories. His stories give readers insight into how the people of Dubai try to adjust their traditional values based on family relationships and Islam to the expectations of modern life in the emirates and represent the realist genre of Gulf literature. In the title story, "The Wink of the Mona Lisa," a husband reminisces to his wife about their first meeting and how shocked and excited he was when she winked at him. Her forwardness attracted him and led him to pursue her hand in marriage. The young woman keeps silent as she recalls that evening and the particle of dust in her eye that caused her to keep blinking all night.

The remaining Emirati or Kuwaiti writers have had one or more of their stories appear in either Western anthologies of Middle Eastern literature or in one of the two government collections.[2] Two Emirati writers whose works have made it into anthologies are Abd al-Hameed Ahmad (1957–), who was self-educated, and Sara al-Nawwaf (1965–), who represents the next generation of Emirati writers. Ahmad became the deputy head of the Union of Writers in the UAE and is known as one of the major short story writers in the Gulf region. His stories depict both the tragic and the comic consequences for people's lives of the discovery of oil and the sudden wealth it brought. His story "Khalalah SEL" focuses on a simple man, Khalalah (Arabic for a green, unripe palm fruit), who works with his donkey, Massoud, to eke out a meager but satisfying existence carrying loads for others. As the oil wealth hits his community, his work vanishes. He goes to the government ministry for help and is given a job as a school caretaker. Massoud carries him every day to his new job. More change is to come, however. His house is confiscated to build a road, and he receives millions in compensation. This sudden turn of fate leaves him bewildered and lost, and the banker steps in to help him purchase a new palace for a home and a new Mercedes SEL to carry him about town, as benefits his new social standing. Massoud is left to wander as the car now drives Khalalah every day to his job as the school caretaker. The story ends with Khalalah waking to a stench coming from a new building near his new home. On investigation, the corpse of a donkey is discovered there. The donkey got stuck between two walls and was unable to get out. The story ends, "Khalalah faced the morning and the people with the same glazed glance and silent absence of mind."

Sara al-Nawwaf received a degree in psychology from UAE University, wrote television scripts and plays for children, and worked as a librarian in Dubai. Her story "Surprise" was first published in 1986 in a collection put out by the Union of Writers in the emirate. This story is a good example of literature that casts a critical eye on the contradictions of women's lives in modern UAE. The main character, Nura, is a young woman whose father insists she stay in seclusion in the family home. Nura uses new technology, the telephone, to begin talking with a young man, Khalid, who dials her number because he is bored. Their relationship grows over several months of phone calls, and eventually, they agree to meet in person. Nura is accompanied to a park by her friend Salwa, who is totally veiled because her husband requires it. At the park, the girls learn that Khalid is actually Salwa's husband, Abdullah. The story ends with Salwa throwing her veil on the ground and storming off, as her husband and friend stand speechless.

Kuwaiti Layla al-Uthman (1945–) is considered a leading female writer in the Arabian Peninsula. She had no education beyond secondary school but read widely in Arabic and Western literature. Her story "The Picture" looks at modernization and women's lives from a different angle. Rather than the woman being betrayed by a man, her main character, a woman of forty-five, decides to be unfaithful to her husband after a party to celebrate her birthday. She feels less attractive than her husband and doubts he really loves her. She gets in a car and drives to the market to have an "experience." There she sees a woman whom she thinks she recognizes. Suddenly she remembers her son sending her a photo of a middle-aged woman with whom he had an affair. As the woman's picture and her own face blend together in her mind, she returns to her car and goes home.

In "Zahra Enters the Neighborhood," al-Uthman explores how people can be duped by beauty. A beautiful stranger, Zahra, comes to a neighborhood and gradually wins the trust of all the people who live there. Only one woman, Um Mohammed, sees her as she sits in her doorway at night to take the fresh sea air and understands what is happening and tries to warn others. Soon, the local residents of the neighborhood are displaced as Zahra's family members buy all the houses in the neighborhood. In the end, the neighbors finally heed Um Mohammed's warnings, but it is too late.

Emirati Salma Matar Saif's work is one prominent example of the genre of magical realism in Gulf writing. In her story "The Serpent," the narrator is taken to a strange place, where he meets a man who tells him that he is married to a djinn. After divulging his secret, the man suddenly becomes worried that his djinn wife will be angry with him and leave him. The narrator himself ends up caught in the spirit world, turned into a serpent. As he slithers away, he hears the man, weeping and lost.

The first short story written by a Bahraini was Mahmud Yusuf's short story "A Confused Woman," which appeared in November 1941. The first piece of fiction written by a woman was the short story "Oblivion Swallowed Her," written by Muzah al-Zayd and published in the newspaper *al-Watan* in 1955. Bahrain's earliest writers were influenced by the romanticism then common in other parts of the Arab world (Ramsay 2005, 134). By the 1960s, Bahraini writers were turning to realism in their work, followed by social criticism in the 1970s. More recently, Bahraini writers, like Farid Ramadan (1961–) and 'Abd al-Qadir 'Aqil, use surrealism in their writing.[3] Ramadan's work, *Between This Life and the Next: A Travelling Star* (2000), is set in a village, after the oil boom, and focuses on a young girl born into a family of grave diggers. Ramadan uses his heroine, Sarra, to explore both the themes of coming to awareness of sexuality and how to deal with death and possible afterlife. In *The Palm of Maryam's Hand* (1997), 'Aqil links the life of his young male character to the 1967 Arab-Israeli War and its aftermath. The young boy had a twin sister who died—or did she? Throughout the book, it is unclear who is dead and who is living.

Fawzia Rashid (Bahrain) has been writing fiction since 1977. Her first novel, *The Siege*, published in 1983, was considered by some critics to be the real beginning of fictional writing in Bahrain. She has worked as a journalist, writing both literary and critical pieces for Gulf and Arab presses. Her second novel, *The Metamorphoses of a Strange Knight in Arabising Lands* (published in 1990), was rewritten four times over five years. In this novel, she deliberately broke from the more common themes seen in other women's writing, focused as they were on family and children, to compose a work that focused on the breadth of Arab history.

A remarkable feature of modern Qatari literature is that there are almost as many women writing as there are men (Ramsay 2002–2003, 372).[4] Amina al-Imadi's short story "The Cold Sun" looks at the breakdown of the family, as elderly people end up confined to institutions instead of being cared for by their relatives. Kulthum Jabar's 1981 story "A New Birth" tells of a young woman whose family takes her to Paris. She sneaks out of her hotel room and roams the streets of the city, sleeping in a park. Waking, she realizes she wants to return to the hotel and her family. In Noura al-Saad's work "The Dream and the Waiting," a working mother who had aspired to be a painter but received no support for her dream decides not to let her dream die and purchases paints and starts to work. In many of these works, the writers focus on a restructuring of the norms of sexual behavior and the role and position of women in society.

Oman was the last country in which a modern literary movement developed. The first works of fiction by an Omani author ('Abd Allah bin Muhammad at-Ta'i) were published in 1981, eight years after his death in 1973. The first prose collection, *The Green Mountain*, written by Saif al-Rahbi, appeared in 1983. Female author Badriyya ash-Shihhī is credited with creating the first real Omani novel, *Treading around the Embers*, in 1999.[5] Omani writers Hamad Rashid and Muhammad al-Yahiya'i provide excellent examples of the third genre of Gulf writing—the modernist, condensed, "very short" story.

Rashid is a master of this form. One of his shortest stories, "A Wound," is 247 words long. In her discussion of his prize-winning work "Azzān," Gail Ramsay points out that it is only 312 words, covering a little over two pages. The brief story tells us about the young man Azzān, who rides out with other men of his tribe to avert an attack by the Portuguese. His father had been killed in an earlier battle. Brief, detached sentences propel the reader forward; words have multiple meanings and evoke other connections. The reader must participate in constructing the text (Ramsay 2006b, 271–273). One could well imagine that an English-language translation of this piece would end up much longer than the original because the English-language reader would need considerable guidance and explanation in how to complete the gaps.

Muhammad al-Yahiya'i writes criticism of how modern life and wealth have disrupted traditional ways of living. In his story "He Went Far Away," a man moves to live away from the city because he cannot cope with the noise, corruption, and activity, only to be shot dead by a stray bullet from a hunter's rifle. In another of his stories, "Sabah," the heroine of that name wakes one morning to discover she is no longer a girl, but has become a man overnight. She remembers a nightmare in which a creature carried her off. Having no men's clothing, she/he dresses as usual and takes the bus to work. From that day on, he/she lives life in a normal manner, as if nothing changed (Ramsay 2006a).

Theater and Drama

Drama, as it developed in the West, is a modern introduction to the Middle East. Two related forms did develop in the Islamic world—the *maqāmah* and the shadow play (*khayāl al-zill*). The *maqāmah* tells the tale of a ne'er-do-well character who impersonates others to earn his living. It mixes both narrative prose and dramatic elements. The shadow play, performed using puppets, whose shadows are cast onto a screen, comes closest to Western drama, as the puppet characters act out various tales. Shadow theater continued to develop in the Middle East, incorporating satire, comedy, and burlesque. Western-style drama entered Middle Eastern literature due to colonial contact. As European influence spread throughout the region, theaters and opera houses were opened in Cairo, Alexandria, and Beirut. Both of the early founders of Arabic drama were inspired by the Italian opera and were influenced by the comedies of the French playwright Molière (Badawi 1992, 339).

The key figure in the development of modern Arabic drama is the Egyptian playwright Tawfiq al-Hakim, who wrote and published more than eighty plays and established drama as a recognized literary form (Altoma 2005). Al-Hakim's work, representing one strand within modern Arabic drama, was mainly written in classical Arabic so that his plays could be performed throughout the Arabic world and appeal to all Arab audiences, regardless of their national origins. A second strand developed, consisting of writers who wrote in the vernacular—colloquial speech and regional Arabic dialects. These plays were seen as more realistic presentations of people's lives, but, unlike al-Hakim's work, these plays cannot always travel across geographical boundaries, thus limiting readership. In addition, fewer of these works have been translated because they require fluency in both classical and colloquial Arabic.

Drama in the Arab Gulf states is a twentieth-century innovation, developing first in Kuwait and Bahrain. The first well-known Kuwaiti playwright was Muhammad al-Nashmi, who produced over twenty plays between 1956 and 1962. His plays drew on comic themes taken from real life. The plays were charged with social and personal criticism and were improvised and thus not committed to writing (Badawi 1992). His work left a deep impression on later writers, especially Saqr ar-Rushud.

Saqr ar-Rushud (1944?–1978) was born in Kuwait and received degrees in commerce and economics from Kuwait University. His promising career in the theater was cut short by an early death. Ar-Rushud wrote a series of plays that focused on the changing relationship between fathers and their children as Kuwait modernized. Drawing his materials from situations he saw occurring around him, ar-Rushud wrote about the clash between tradition and modernity, especially focusing on attitudes about women. His best-known plays include *I and Fate* (1964), *The Big Fang* (1965), *The Mud* (1965), and *The Barricade* (1966).

The Mud is considered one of his best works. The play follows the story of an older merchant who has taken a beautiful young second wife because he wants a son. His first wife has left him and taken all their daughters but one with her. The daughter who remains, herself a plain woman, married a handsome man who wanted her for her money and who has brought shame on the family by his extravagant spending. The merchant hates the husband and wants his daughter to abort the child she is carrying. To make matters worse, the daughter knows that her husband does not want her because he is carrying on an affair with her father's young wife and is trying to get the wife to kill the old man. The merchant, in despair at how his life has deteriorated, takes his own life. On his death, the faithless husband and young wife both leave. Left behind is the merchant's daughter in the company of a faithful household servant. The play ends with the servant lecturing the corpse about the undeserved wealth of the rich and the fate of the poor who actually produce the wealth.

Collaborating with ar-Rushud in pushing Kuwaiti theater forward, 'Abd al-'Aziz al-Surayyi' (1939–) has moved into the forefront of drama in Kuwait. Al-Surayyi' is known for his dramatic experimentation and his success in representing the social and psychological changes that sudden oil wealth wrought on the inhabitants of the country. He became the secretary general of the 'Abd al-'Aziz al-Babitain Prize for Poetry and Poetic Criticism and has done considerable service for the cause of poetry in the Arab world. Two of his plays received considerable attention: *Money and Souls* (1969–1970) and *The Bird Has Flown* (1971). In the first work, he wrote about a man who became wealthy by selling his house to the government. With his newfound wealth, he became a different person—buying new clothes, taking a new foreign wife, and finally, denying his family by accusing them of attempting to defraud him.

The Bird Has Flown was first performed under the direction of Saqr ar-Rushud in 1972. The performers used a broad Kuwaiti dialect in the performance, but when al-Surayyi' published it, he made the language more comprehensible without resorting to using classical Arabic. This play juxtaposes British culture and lifestyles with traditional Arabic culture. One of the main characters is an older wealthy man, who, in his youth, was a sailor involved in the pearl trade. On one of his voyages to India, he married a second wife and had a son. They divorced soon after his son was born, and his ex-wife took his son to England to live, and the man lost contact with them. The play revolves around the lost son, Yusuf, coming to Kuwait to meet his father and family for the first time. Yusuf upsets the balance within the family by having a love affair with the daughter of his uncle, who was meant to be his stepbrother's wife. When his affair comes out, he flees back to England, rather than marry the young woman, and leaves behind a shamed woman and a destroyed family.

In Bahrain, one sees the same themes of social injustice, patriarchal despotism, and children futilely revolting against coercive parents emerging in the dramatic works being written (Badawi 1992, 397). In the work *Steadfast* by Sultan Salim (from the 1970s), the theme of social injustice is the focus as the employees of a department threaten to strike against their abusive civil servant boss, Salman. In his private life, Salman is a slave to his mistress, giving her whatever she wants. When an old tenant comes to pay his rent and reports that he only has part of the rent, Salman threatens to evict him. The mistress takes pity on him and gives him the remainder of the money he needs. In the end, the employees lose their will to strike because they are poor and cannot afford to lose their jobs. However, the young man who was the leader still goes ahead with his own decision to strike, refusing to be bribed by Salman. At the end of the play, an earthquake breaks an island in two, and a young woman wearing traditional Bahraini dress scolds all those who squander wealth and deny the rights of workers and the needy, warning that one day, they will awaken.

The first theater troupes in Kuwait started in 1938 in the schools, with students producing plays under the direction of their foreign teachers, who came with the Arab teachers' mission. Plays focused on Islamic themes or taught important values. By 1940, there were theater troupes in four schools. In October 1961, the Ministry of Social Affairs invited Egyptian Zaki Tulaymat to come to Kuwait to provide recommendations about how to promote Kuwaiti theater. Tulaymat formed the Arab Theater troupe that same year. Al-Nashmi formed the Al-Kashaf National Troupe (later known as the Popular Theater Troupe); al-Rashud formed the National Theater (which later disbanded). The Arabian Gulf Troupe and the Kuwaiti Theater (also formed by al-Nashmi after he resigned from the Popular Theater) round out the theatrical troupes in Kuwait.

Once the oil money began flowing, almost every state in the Gulf built its own theaters, and developments similar to those seen in Kuwait were repeated elsewhere in the region. Qatar built a National Theater that boasted computerized lighting systems, translation facilities, and an orchestra pit, which could be raised or lowered electronically. Sharjah ran a state-sponsored theater workshop, which offered courses on acting, writing, and production and which produced an upsurge in both locally written plays and in foreign plays adapted for the Gulf stage (Bulloch 1984, 151). The Information Ministry in Bahrain announced in April 2008 that they would build a theater in every governorate to rejuvenate theater in the country.

MEDIA

A major issue for the press in the region is the issue of censorship. Every Gulf country has restrictions on reporting that is critical of the ruling families, whether those restrictions are formally enshrined in law or simply a matter of self-censorship. Bahrain's 1965 press law allows no reports that are harmful to national security or offensive to the ruling family's reputation. In

Kuwait, a 1961 law established fines and prison for publishing material critical of the government, although the law was rarely used and Kuwait was known for press freedom. In 1986, however, the government established new restrictions to quell political dissent. In the aftermath of the Iraq War, the Kuwaiti government lifted censorship in 1992, but restrictions still remain on reporters. In the UAE, press members are technically free, as long as they do not criticize the government or ruling families. Qatar formally lifted press censorship in 1995, but the press self-censor and are careful not to report material that would be critical of the ruling family or about religious issues. In Oman, the press law of 1984 gave the government the right to try and to imprison journalists without having to give any reasons. It is not uncommon for journalists throughout the region to be placed under arrest for weeks or months at a time.

Because of pervasive press censorship (not just in the Gulf states, but throughout the Arab world) and examples of biased or plainly misleading reporting on major world events (such as Egyptians being told they were winning the 1967 Arab-Israeli War when they had already lost it), many Arab citizens have learned to distrust what they read in the media. Instead, they turn to the markets and the mosques and to informal, word-of-mouth channels to find out what is really happening in their countries. Radio Monte Carlo, the Voice of America, and the BBC gained in popularity with their Arabic-language broadcasts. However, as Western-owned stations, they were still subject to skepticism. Television remains more important than print media as the major source for news due to still high illiteracy rates in the countries of the region. Satellite dishes are inexpensive and have become popular wedding gifts. It's not uncommon to see a traditional tent in the desert with a satellite dish nearby.

Bahrain is the base for the pan-Arab satellite broadcaster MBC. Television and radio stations are state run by the Bahrain Radio and Television Corporation. They operate five television networks and five radio channels (a general one, one focusing on cultural and local programming, a sports channel, a Quran program, and an English-language channel). A private radio station, Sawt al-Ghad, began broadcasting in 2005 but was shut down by the government in 2006 due to irregularities. There are five privately published daily papers, two of which are published in English: *Akhbar al-Khaleej, al-Wasat, al-Ayam*, the *Bahrain Tribune*, and the *Gulf Daily News*.

Kuwaiti journalists have greater freedom in reporting than do their counterparts in other Gulf countries, but they still must not criticize the ruling family. Their press law also forbids insulting religious references. Satellite dishes are popular, allowing citizens to watch pan-Arab television stations and not just the local Kuwaiti channels. Radio Kuwait and Kuwaiti TV are state run. The television service features three networks and a satellite channel, while the radio station broadcasts programming in Arabic and English. There are two private television stations: al-Rai, which broadcasts via satellite, and Flash TV. There is also a private, music-based FM radio station called Marina FM. There are five privately published daily papers, two of which are published in English: *al-Watan*, *al-Qabas*, *al-Rai al-Amm*, the *Arab Times*, and the *Kuwait Times*.

In Oman, Oman television and Radio Oman are both state run. Satellite dishes are permitted, and viewers can capture channels from nearby countries like Yemen and the UAE. The radio station broadcasts in both Arabic and English. In addition to state-run radio, there are two private radio channels broadcasting Arabic music and one private FM channel broadcasting in English. There are four newspapers, two published in English: *al-Watan* and *Oman Daily* (in Arabic) and the *Oman Observer* and the *Times of Oman* (in English).

The UAE created an Electronic Commerce and Media Zone Authority in 2000 to attract international media outlets to the emirates. Dubai Media City has attracted major media conglomerates like Reuters and Sony as well as publishers, artists, and writers. Satellite broadcaster MBC moved its offices from London to Dubai. Television broadcasters include Dubai Media Incorporated, Abu Dhabi TV, Ajman TV, Sharjah TV, and MBC. There are seven different radio stations in operation, and among them, they broadcast in Hindi, Urdu, Malayalam, English, and Arabic. There is one privately owned Arabic-language newspaper, *al-Bayan*, and four English-language papers, the *Gulf News*, the *Khaleej Times* (privately owned), the *National*, and *Emirates Business 24/7*.

Qatar's launch in 1996 of the twenty-four-hour satellite news channel al-Jazeera vaulted the country onto the international media scene. The station is partially owned by the government and partially by private citizens. It claims an Arabic-speaking audience of over 40 million people. In 2006, al-Jazeera launched its English-language news broadcast, the first Middle East–based news and current events channel.

Al-Jazeera benefited from its beginnings from Western inabilities to understand the cultural climate of the Arabian Peninsula. The BBC had made a deal with Saudi-owned satellite television company Orbit to start an Arabic-language television channel. Started in 1994, the BBC-Orbit arrangement fell apart when its Saudi financiers were angered by programming that was broadcast critical of the Saudi government. As that venture ended, 120 of the Arab journalists, broadcasters, and technicians, who were out of work, accepted jobs with al-Jazeera, giving the new station a well-trained and professional work force from its beginnings.

Al-Jazeera began broadcasting six hours a day from the Arabsat satellite on a weak Ku-band transponder. Within a year, they were broadcasting twelve hours a day, but their signal was so weak that very few satellite dish owners could actually capture the signal. In July 1997, a French station broadcasting on Arabsat on a coveted C-band transponder made a fatal error. Their technicians broadcast thirty minutes of a hard-core pornographic film, instead of the thirty minutes of children's educational programming that was scheduled. The French company was gone, and al-Jazeera took their spot broadcasting on the stronger frequency in November 1997, streaming seventeen hours of programming a day.

Al-Jazeera captured international attention for its coverage of ongoing conflicts in Afghanistan and Iraq and its broadcasts of messages from Osama bin Laden. However, it captured notice in the Arab world initially for its talk shows (Miles 2005, 37). The shows tackle political, social, economic, and religious topics, using face-to-face interview, documentary, and live debate formats. The talk shows also offered the possibility for viewers to call in and join the discussion. Unlike other stations that used this format, al-Jazeera's callers were aired completely live, with no screening or time delay.

The station has rapidly expanded since its beginnings—broadcasting twenty-four hours and adding an Arabic-language Web site, a sports channel, and its English channel.[6] When it first began broadcasting, it was available only in the Middle East. Its reach is now global. It has established a reputation for itself as free and open media. Its reporting has brought down on its head the wrath of both Arab and Western governments, particularly in its early years. As it became clear that the station was not going away, the number of complaints has dwindled. Instead, many Arab governments have tried to copy the success of al-Jazeera. Al-Jazeera remade the face of television in the Arab world (Miles 2005, 335).

In addition to al-Jazeera, Qatar TV is state owned and broadcasts Arabic and English channels as well as a Quran channel and a satellite channel. Qatar Broadcasting Services, the radio station, is also state owned and broadcasts in Arabic, English, Urdu, and French. There are three Arabic-language newspapers (*al-Watan, al-Rayah*, and *al-Sharq*) and three English-language papers (the *Gulf Times*, the *Qatar Tribune*, and the *Peninsula*).

NOTES

1. Short stories in English by Gulf writers can be found in the following sources listed in the bibliography: Clerk and Siegel (1995), "Khalalah SEL" (UAE); Gerrard and McCarthy (1993), "Surprise" (UAE); and Cohen-Mor (1993), "The Picture" (Kuwait). There are two volumes in English of stories from the UAE by al-Murr (1991,

1994) and two collections of short stories from the UAE and Kuwait published by the respective governments: Tahboub (2000) and al-Sanousi (2001). Poetry in English by Gulf writers can be found in the following sources: Asfour (1988), Bahrain; Obank and Shimon (2001), Bahrain, UAE, Oman, Kuwait; Handal (2001), Bahrain, Kuwait, Qatar, UAE; Jayyusi (1987), Bahrain, Oman, Kuwait; and Fairbairn and al-Gosaibi (1989), Oman, Kuwait, Qatar, Bahrain, and UAE.

2. These writers include Kuwaiti authors Sulaiman al-Shatti (1943–), Sulaiman al-Khulaifi (1946–), Thurayya al-Baqsomi (1952), Waleed al-Rujeib (1954–), Hamad al-Hamad (1954–), and Mohammed al-Ajmi (1956–). Among the Emirati authors are Maryam Juma'a Faraj (who writes about the lives of Indian expatriate workers), Suad al-Oraimi, Amina Bu Shihab, Asma'a al-Zarouni, Fatma Mohammed, Shaikha al-Nakhi, Salha Ghabish, Naser al-Thaheri, Naser Jubran, Ibrahim al-Mubarak, Hareb al-Thahri, and Abdul Hamid Ahmad. See Michalak-Pikulska (1998) for a study about Kuwaiti literature from 1929 to 1995.

3. Other Bahraini writers include Amin Salih (1950–), Muhammad Abd al-Malik, Abd al-Qadir 'Aqil (1949–), Ali Abd Allah Khalifah (1950–), Fawziyyah Muhammad al-Sanadi (1956–), and Khalaf Ahmad Khalaf.

4. Qatari writers include Jamal Fayez, Abdul Qadir al-Emiri, and Khalid S. al-Khater. Prominent women writers include Kulthum Jabar (1960–), Nour al-Saad, Loulowah al-Misnid, Zahra Yousif al-Malki, Bahia 'Abdul Rahman al-Baker, Amina al-'Imadi, and Norah al-Khater.

5. Omani writers include Saud al-Mudhaffar (1953–), Ahmad Bilal (1951–), Hamad Rashid (1960–), Muhammad al-Yahiya'i, and Ali al-Ma'mari. Besides ash-Shihi, other prominent women writers include Badriyya al-Wahaybi, Tahira bint 'Abd al-Khaliq al-Lawati, Bushra Khalfan Wahaybi, and Khawla Hamdan. See Michalak-Pikulska (2002) for a study of Omani literature from 1970 to 2000.

6. The station's English-language Web site is available at http://english.aljazeera.net/.

4

Settlement, Architecture, and Material Culture

INTRODUCTION

THE HARSH, BARREN climate, a paucity of natural materials, and social and religious practices dictated early architectural, material, and aesthetic practices. Before the acquisition of oil wealth and its associated large-scale urbanization, nearly all material culture was useful as well as aesthetically appealing. Women wore silver and gold jewelry because it was attractive but also because it warded off evil and had a central role in marriage customs. Housing structures relied on decorative ventilation systems, the main purpose of which was to capture cooling breezes. Material possessions were often limited, given the small size of houses, the need for mobility in Bedouin tents, and the lack of disposable wealth. While there is a minimal amount of architectural and material cultural tradition, it does not mean that people had no appreciation for aesthetics. Rather, there were limited materials, time, and options for decorative display. Contemporary architecture in the Gulf reflects a more elaborate and global aesthetic, yet also reflects regional values. The utilization of local and Islamic motifs, archways, carved gypsum panels, and calligraphy pays homage to past traditions.

Today, the Arab Gulf states are studies in rapid, modern urban development. Nearly all cities have experienced explosive growth since the 1980s. New city centers erupt across the desert, punctuating the landscape with gleaming steel and glass skyscrapers, freeways, construction sites, and green park areas. Alongside this expansive development are clusters of older buildings with traditional architecture; mud houses and coral-block historic forts stand in sharp juxtaposition to modern buildings of concrete and steel. For some, this mixing of traditional and contemporary architectural forms exemplifies a vibrant region that seeks to balance increased demand for modern urban living with historic preservation. For others, especially those interested in Gulf heritage, recent reconstructions of so-called traditional buildings are strange, minimal efforts to stave off the erasure of the material signs of past Gulf life.

As lifestyle habits have changed and mass-produced goods are readily available in shopping malls, few people make handicrafts to supply items used daily such as weavings for carpets and seating cushions or silver filigree work for jewelry and weaponry. Some artisans dedicate themselves to keeping alive past craft traditions, but generally, folk materials such as weavings, traditionally styled jewelry, and *khanjars* (sheathed daggers) are produced en masse for the tourist market. Antiques are readily available in stores and *suqs* (such as the Nizwa *suq* in Oman), which offer carved wooden doors extracted from demolished houses (often now fashioned into coffee tables) and antique camel saddlebags sold as seat cushions or satchels. Some traditional bodily art practices, such as the application of complex henna tattoos, have moved out of the house and can now be found in most Arab and Indian salons, carrying on a tradition of decoration commonly used for weddings and holidays.

Omani chest with handmade grommets reflecting Indian style, al-Batinah region, Oman. Courtesy of Elizabeth Faier.

SETTLEMENT: FROM DESERT TO CITY

It is difficult to speak of an urban past even with the centrality of the Gulf in the former pearl trade. Today's major cities, such as Dubai, were, in the nineteenth and early twentieth centuries, small communities built along waterfronts. There are a few exceptions, however. Old Kuwait town, for instance, had sixty thousand residents in 1930. Located along the waterfront and stretching inland, it was surrounded by a fortification wall. Inside the walled city were residences, gardens, Islamic and Christian cemeteries, and public buildings. Primarily built from mud brick, it had little structural organization that would look familiar to today's town plans. Manama in Bahrain is also an historic city. *Al-Bab al-Bahrain* (the gate of Bahrain), built in 1945 along the harbor, signals the importance of the city both in trading and for the British, who moved their main naval base for the Gulf region to Bahrain in the 1930s and 1940s. Likewise, Muharraq, the former capital of Bahrain, which is today a world apart from modern Manama, was once a thriving community.

Most of the accelerated growth in Gulf cities like Kuwait City, Manama, Muscat, Dubai, Abu Dhabi, and Doha directly stems from the discovery of oil. Earlier settlements were either tied to freshwater springs and water areas or found dotted across vast expanses of desert. In both cases, little evidence remains of these communities as most structures were not built for permanence or have been cleared for modern development. However, the need for protection in past centuries remains evident in the many fortresses and watchtowers that stand out across the landscape, bearing testament to the need of early residents to safeguard the seas and, in places like Oman and the United Arab Emirates (UAE), the mountains. Unlike the heterogeneity of modern centers, where neighborhoods interweave with commercial districts and neighbors are often strangers, early settlements were more homogenous, organized politically, economically, and spatially according to tribal membership, loyalty, and migration needs. In general, people lived quite simply, with family as neighbors, little permanent settlement or architecture, and few material possessions.

As nomads, Bedouin life was fundamentally mobile, revolving around the search for water and the tending of animals. Bedouins spent long periods of time in oases, where they had access to freshwater, usually through underground springs, and date palms, which supplied everything from food to building materials. Water was a major source of life. It could be directed from springs to settlements or drawn from wells, serving everyday needs and irrigating the date groves that are a hallmark of oasis communities. Animals were also of paramount importance, especially goats and camels, which could provide milk for drinking, hair for weaving, and, when slaughtered, food for eating. The fortitude of the camel is legendary; its ability to withstand long periods without water and food made it an especially useful animal in the harsh climate of the Gulf. While the camel can drink up to twenty-five gallons of water at one time, its body regulates temperature to avoid sweating and thus conserve water. It is incorrect to think that it stores water in its hump; rather, the hump on its back is a food reservoir, and a floppy and weak hump signifies malnutrition and not a lack of water.

Given their nomadic lifestyle and appreciation for large amounts of living space, it is difficult to speak about Bedouin settlement before urbanization; rather, Arab tribesmen moved freely across the peninsula, often crossing what are now the defined borders of nation-states. Reasons for migration varied, but in general, as the seasons changed, people needed to move to areas that would afford subsistence. Most tribal groups had a number of known areas where they could find food and water, and these places punctuated migration routes. Although the image of nomads wandering the desert is powerful, it is important to note that tribes owned specific territory and oases—and that tribal groups shared the knowledge of which tribe was in what area. When tribes crossed into lands controlled by other tribal groups, they were sometimes granted water rights, but this depended on the good will of the sheikhs. Today, oases continue to be valued. Not only are they sites where Bedouins lived for extended periods and thus have special significance for people of those tribes, but also, they provide respite from the harsh climate, with temperatures many degrees cooler than the surrounding desert.

Some Bedouin moved to cities and adopted lifestyles different from their nomadic ancestors. In Kuwait, *hadar* is the term that denotes settled traders; however, the *hadar* were originally Bedouin who moved to the water for trade reasons. Others—Persians, Indians, and Arab-African slaves—also settled the coastal areas of the Gulf states in the nineteenth century, seeking new opportunity in the trade routes that extended across the Arabian Gulf and Indian Ocean. These groups settled in neighborhoods, bringing with them language, tradition, and architecture. For instance, along the creek in Dubai, a sizeable number of traders from Bastak, Iran, settled what is now known as the Bastakiya neighborhood.

Identity classifications that stem from early settlement patterns remain important today. Ancestry signifies subtle differences in everything from clothing to language but, more important, determines one's legitimacy in making claims of tribal origins. For example, among Qatari citizens, three categories are commonly used: *arab,* which refers to those of Bedouin or tribal ancestry; *ajam,* which indicates those of Persian origin; and *abd,* which signifies those who were slaves. While all are citizens, the Bedouin roots of the state create closer ties of belonging for Arab groups than others.

Despite state attempts to foster nationalism across ethnic and religious divisions, tribalism continues to play a large role in settlement patterns and day-to-day activities. For example, the UAE seeks to inculcate an Emirati identity and encourages Emiratis to freely move to Ajman, Dubai, or any of the seven emirates that compose the UAE. Yet most Emiratis feel allegiance with their emirate not only because of sentiments of place, but also, and perhaps more important, because they associate place with tribal authority. Each emirate was initially settled by a tribal group or its clan. Moreover, people prefer to reside with or near their extended or larger family, resulting in strong associations between settlement and identity. In the situation of a large family living in two emirates, people identify themselves as the family al-Suweidi from emirate Abu Dhabi.

As many states root their claims to place through tribal networks, belonging takes on paramount importance. While states such as Qatar and the UAE extol their Bedouin pasts in the foundation of the nation-state, other states point to other settlement patterns. Bedouins, for instance, settled Kuwait, but they adopted the identity of *hadar*, or settled merchants, given the early urban fabric of the area. Today, some *hadar* suggest that recent Bedouin citizens, or *bedu*, are opportunistic foreigners who moved to Kuwait because the government, also *bedu*, provides them with benefits (Longva 2006). The question of identity as it relates to settlement emerges in vernacular debates over who has the right—or greater right—to the heritage of place as well as the symbols employed by the state. Other identity-settlement categories, such as stateless Bedouin (those without nationality papers) and expatriates (workers who have moved to the Gulf and comprise the majority of the population in many states), further complicate rights of residence and settlement.

Given the harsh climate, proximity to water was and continues to be of utmost importance—seas and creeks provide outlets for trading, while freshwater springs and wells supply drinking and irrigation water for residents. Folkloric stories illustrate the importance of water. One story that narrates the founding of Abu Dhabi tells of how members of the Bani Yas tribe, who were staying at oases in Liwa, on the edge of the Rub al-Khali, or "Empty Quarter" (a vast, barren area of high sand dunes), left in search of water. After many days of travel, they saw gazelles in the distance and followed them, despite their realization that if they did not soon find a source of water, they would die. When they awoke at dawn on the following day, the gazelles were gone, but the men found themselves at a freshwater spring. This spring enabled the settlement of the island city of Abu Dhabi, which means "father of gazelles."

Throughout parts of the Gulf, natural springs and mountain runoff feed oases, or lush areas of growth, where palm trees and agriculture can thrive.

While these oases provided cooler temperatures and water for survival, people also diverted water from other sources, enabling groups to live in what would otherwise be arid conditions. To bring water from mountain wadis (valleys) and underground springs, trenches were dug deep in the earth, or aboveground channels were created through which the water would flow from its source. This system is called a *falaj* (singular) and is most common in Oman and the UAE. *Aflaj* (plural) denotes the entire system, including the source of water, its conveyance (either in aboveground troughs or underground tunnels), and distribution. Once the water reached the community, people drew on it for their needs, and the remainder was diverted to agricultural areas. The *aflaj* is of utmost importance to people and conveys a great deal of social significance, as evidenced in its administration and place in heritage areas. In Oman, it continues to play a major role in the distribution of water in both settled and agricultural areas. *Aflaj* have been in use for over a thousand years, although most of those currently in use are from more recent centuries.

Settlements were fundamentally compact, minimizing the distance among core features of the built environment, which included housing clusters, mosques, schools, *suqs*, and fortresses. When settling an area, people constructed their houses in clusters, creating de facto homogenous quarters with shared ethnic, religious, familial, and cultural commonalities. In Kuwait City, the *hadar* settled closest to the port, while Bedouin settled outlying areas, a pattern that remains today, although some areas now have mixed populations. Quarters physically circumscribed community and kin relations that were central to daily life, providing safety and support when needed. Often, these quarters would be named after the family that resided there or the original locale of residents. The irregular, narrow, and winding pedestrian streets that snaked between the houses not only defined quarters of the city, but also provided shady relief from the hot sun, as the houses threw shadows across the open areas.

Historically, every community had a central or great mosque as well as smaller mosques that were closer to housing cells. In cities with heterogeneous populations (even if people lived in homogenous quarters), people primarily attended the mosque of their sect and/or ethnic community, which was usually the local neighborhood mosque. If a community had a madrassa, or religious school, it was located near or attached to the mosque. *Suqs* were also centers of daily life, a place for trade as well as for social exchange for men who drank coffee in coffeehouses located within the *suq*. In the *suq*, nearly all daily necessities could be found such as copper and brass wares, textiles, spices, food, animals, and clothing. Finally, fortresses anchored large settlements, providing safety in time of war as well as housing important sheikhs and their families.

THE MODERN CITY

Contemporary Gulf cities resemble other modern international cities, especially those in Asia, with enormous skyscrapers, bustling commercial centers, and wide highways bursting with traffic. Yet they also share commonalities with older settlements: housing quarters with homogenous (or nearly so) populations, a centrality of markets, and a centrality of religious and government institutions. Nearly every residence has a mosque within a few hundred meters. Forts and watchtowers (reconstructed or their remains) stand in many cities, although now they house museums and are part of larger heritage displays. With increased population numbers, primarily due to migration, residential areas are becoming more mixed and the variety of housing is greater. Finally, *suq*s still exist, but usually for specific goods such as gold, animals, and food; they are quickly being replaced by air-conditioned shopping malls that cater to both local and expatriate populations. In this context of transformation from local settlement to modern, global environment, many local municipalities are seeking ways to maintain and foster aspects of Gulf heritage.

In the last forty years, settlement has increased across the Gulf, practically transforming Kuwait, Bahrain, and Qatar into city-states and the UAE and Oman into states with large cities that continue to experience population explosion. Unlike eras of the past, in which Bedouin maintained a nomadic lifestyle and merchants settled coastal areas, today's Gulf is primarily urbanized and diverse, with upward of 80 percent of the population living in cities. While people still identify as Bedouin, few practice nomadic lifestyles (except for areas of Oman, where Bedouin still engage in trade) and instead reside in or near Gulf cities, maintaining tribal consciousness, linguistic patterns, and relationships. Likewise, classifications such as *hadar/bedu* and *arab/ajam* continue to have currency, but primarily out of ethnic identification, with consequences more for marriage than for residence, because of tight housing markets. Other populations have also joined the workforce, coming from all areas of the globe, especially Southeast Asia, Europe, and the Philippines.

The complex demography of the Gulf states has many consequences for the rhythm of daily life and the spatial distribution of populations and urban centers. While Arabic remains the official language of the Gulf states, English, Urdu, Hindi, and Tagalog are often the languages of daily interaction and are evident on some official signposting on streets and in stores. Many neighborhoods are diverse, with different population groups sharing apartment buildings or having houses in the same complex. In most cities, when the opportunity arises, ethnic groups prefer to reside in their own neighborhoods, and consequently, different urban areas exhibit distinct housing, residence styles, and services. It can usually be assumed that neighborhoods with large walled houses are local (national) neighborhoods, where residents not only prefer large amounts of space, but also require it, according to social custom. Many national families, if they can afford to do so, maintain family farms outside of urban areas, to which members retreat, or they have large outdoor areas at their in-town residences. Expatriates are unable to buy property, except in designated freehold zones, but law is slow to catch up to social practice, and it is unclear what property rights come with ownership. Mixed populations have spurred on government-sponsored programs that seek to integrate locals into the workforce, develop new national housing projects, and establish cultural centers.

The strain of urban living—rising rates of inflation, congestion and traffic woes, ever present construction, increasing education costs, and lack of housing—receives much attention in the popular press. For nationals, the question of available housing is especially pertinent because younger generations question whether they will be able to live near family members. There are a limited number of national housing projects, constructed by state authorities, but the monotony of the housing and the smaller house size (in comparison to other local homes) make them unattractive. Other options exist, including acquiring land and building new houses in areas designated for locals, buying flats in mixed-ethnicity apartment buildings, or remaining with family. As population density increases and the quest for housing intensifies, new neighborhoods regularly crop up on the outskirts of cities. In Muscat, al-Kuwayr is a popular new quarter, while in Dubai, neighborhoods such as al-Warqa'a meet the housing needs of many nationals. These new neighborhoods differ drastically from older, urbanized quarters, namely, because they are far less homogenous than the previous era's quarters and with fewer services. A popular Arabic expression encourages people to choose the neighborhood first (for neighbors), and then the house.

Daily life remains concentrated around the waterfront, only now highrise buildings, public areas, and restaurants replace trade areas, making corniches (waterfront promenades) sites for strolling, vistas, and leisure activities. New downtowns that wheel and deal in international commerce and attract upwardly mobile populations of European or Arab descent are replacing older hubs of economic activity and daily life. These new hubs of business and modern living overshadow previous economic centers, transforming them into alternate business areas with small shops, local commerce, and specific goods. Modern roads, often with ten lanes and multistory overpasses and roundabouts, direct traffic to new economic areas, carving the cities into districts divided by ring roads and main thoroughfares. Older areas especially suffer from congestion as they have high-density housing and narrow streets.

Sheikh Zayed Road near Defense Roundabout, Dubai, UAE. Courtesy of Anders Linde-Laursen.

Large traffic circles, or roundabouts, are ubiquitous across the Gulf, with many cities relying on them to regulate the increasingly high levels of traffic that plague cities. Often, roundabouts are large in breadth, with sufficient room to accommodate three to four lanes of traffic, requiring drivers to carefully navigate lane changes as they move through the circle, often resulting in perilous driving conditions. Roundabouts, especially in Qatar, Oman, and Bahrain, have large public sculptures in their centers—dhows, oyster shells, coffeepots, and chests are commonly used to symbolize Arabian identity and heritage. In Manama and Dubai, large clock tower roundabouts direct traffic. Most cities do not have a physical address system, but instead use landmarks to help residents find desired locations. For example, in Doha, one finds the "Pearl" (a large clamshell with a pearl) and "Dhow" roundabouts, while in Dubai, the "defense" roundabout (for a defensive outpost) continues to be a major marker, even though it is now a flyover without any markings. In this schema, roundabouts and landmarks are key navigational features.

Decorative landscaping around traffic circles, roadside plantings, and public parks are important greening features of the urban environment. Landscape architects transform a barren, arid environment into a tapestry of plants, flowers, ornamental grasses, and palm trees laid out in elaborate geometric and repeating designs. Parks are of high quality, often offering pavilions, grassy

Mercado Mall domed interior, Dubai, UAE. Courtesy of Elizabeth Faier.

areas, jogging trails, and amusement areas. Green areas not only serve to beautify the cityscape, but also provide places for families and friends to gather on weekends. It is quite common to find people relaxing on Friday afternoons on medians and other grassy areas. Some cities, such as Muscat, enhance the natural environment by placing large animal sculptures along causeways. While it is rare to see a live *maha*, or oryx (a type of gazelle), one can see giant statues standing on the tops of mountain wadis across Muscat.

Given high temperatures, harsh sun, and humidity as well as the traffic congestion and expanding city boundaries, shopping malls are quickly displacing *suq*s (markets) for everyday shopping, although people will frequent specialty *suq*s for items such as gold or electronics. The shopping mall is becoming a hallmark of the modern Arab Gulf; in just about every neighborhood across the Gulf, malls of all sizes can be found, many carrying the latest fashions and goods of international brands. For many, shopping or walking around malls consumes large amounts of time as malls are new private-public arenas for social interaction. The blurring between private and public space can be seen in the practices of local women who bare their face in the malls, except when encountering other local men. Then they hold their *shayla*s across their faces, making a barrier and thus preserving modesty. Many cities, especially Dubai, Abu Dhabi, and Doha, are investing in malls of fantastic proportion and design, offering themed environments and leisure activities such as an indoor ski slope (Mall of the Emirates, UAE) or a Venetian canal and gondola system (Bellagio, Qatar). Still, the *suq* has not completely disappeared, but has become integrated within the mall environment. Some malls, such as Madinat Jumeirah in Dubai, a reconstructed citadel complex, seek to recreate elements of traditional *suq*s and feature wide wooden arches and ribbed ceilings that stretch across meandering passageways—only with modern facilities such as air-conditioning and plumbing. Many malls have *suq*-like areas that sell tourist-oriented goods such as carpets, coffeepots, *shisha* pipes, and other items.

As evident in the development of themed mega-malls, new Gulf cities are seeking ways to capture the luxury lifestyle market that centers on uniqueness, consumerism, leisure, and affluence, drawing in the wealthy from neighboring regions as well as from Europe and North America. Nearly every Gulf state, except perhaps Kuwait, is currently developing at least one mega-development project that combines residential, business, and leisure activities in crafted complexes that declare opulence and speak to the residents' status. Entrance into these exclusive development communities comes with residence, which usually means, barring stays at the hotels located there, ownership. Before such development projects, non-passport-holders could not buy property or receive the right of residence without working.

The market for these projects is expansive, with many buyers purchasing their homes before construction begins, making their decisions only on architectural blueprints and the promise of the lifestyle advertised. With ground just broken, international advertising campaigns encouraged investors in the Burj Dubai Project (world's tallest building) to become part of "History Rising." Of all the Gulf cities, Dubai claims the title for the greatest number of extravagant themed projects: Dubailand, the Palm, and the World (artificial islands made of sand in the shape of the world, enabling investors to buy their "country") are simply a few of the many projects. The race to attract investors results in slogans such as "The Palm put Dubai on the map. The World puts the map on Dubai" that call out new opportunities to investors, while, at the same time, informing residents and tourists of the latest (and thus best) new development schemata that not only will change the landscape, but also transform daily life. Dubai is not alone in using big-money development projects to attract wealth and create new urban centers. In Doha, there are the Pearl and Lusail projects; Manama is creating a brand-new harbor called Bahrain Financial Harbor and building Amwaj Islands; and off the coast of Oman, a number of new luxury developments are slated.

With large amounts of desert, Gulf urban planners have ample space to expand cities, yet much development, and thus destruction, occurs within city centers and rewrites land usage patterns to accommodate growing population numbers and needs. In the 1970s and 1980s, many cities leveled historic areas, which were seen as old and decrepit, to make way for new residential and business complexes, while Kuwait City suffered significant damage during the Gulf War. Also, many houses built from the 1950s to the 1970s were demolished as the cement with which they were built was compromised cement and thus too weak to endure the constant challenges brought by sun and salt. The rapid and accelerating pace of Gulf development brings along with it concern about the preservation of the past, especially architectural heritage and traditional ways. As cities morph into global centers with few elements to distinguish them as Gulf or Arab cities, new attention is focused on constructing heritage areas or villages. These so-called villages, often in downtown locations, are reconstructed neighborhoods that preserve architectural styles and residential patterns for locals, expatriates, and tourists to enjoy, especially during festivals, when they come alive with activity, such as Bedouin women weaving carpets or young men performing a traditional stick dance. These areas are not residential neighborhoods, but living history museums that are part of a new heritage trade targeted as much at locals as tourists.

ARCHITECTURE

Islamic architecture embraces an aesthetic built on geometry, symmetry, repetition of patterns, and the contrast between light and dark spaces. For example, repeating archways are a hallmark of Islamic design. When used on a passageway, so the arches are facing outward, they create a covered walkway with shade patterns that change in relation to the position of the sun, creating plays of light and darkness between interior and exterior areas. The importance of geometric design is also evident in the structure of buildings, which tend to be regular, rectangular buildings built around central courtyards. Likewise, building decorations of carved gypsum panels and metal gates showcase complex abstract designs, in which one strand of the design separates into secondary strands that are then woven back into the original design.

While there is a clear Islamic architectural tradition, architectural historians argue whether a distinct tradition of Gulf architectural design exists; rather, when one speaks of traditional architecture, one is referencing nineteenth- and early-twentieth-century structures that were commonly fabricated out of available materials such as palm fronds, coral blocks, and gypsum bricks; in the 1950s, cement replaced gypsum as it was much cheaper. While these structures employ many aspects of Islamic design, they reflect more the availability of materials for construction and the use of the building. Traditional dwelling types directly correlate with settlement patterns and available materials. For the Bedouin, goat hair provided fibers from which they could weave durable tents. Urbanized dwellers constructed homes out of palm fronds and fibers, coral excavated from the sea, and mud blocks from the earth.

Gulf architecture maintains social customs and gender distinctions that are central to tribal society. Throughout the Middle East and, to an extent, the Islamic world, important distinctions are made between private and public spaces, with women traditionally associated with the former and men with the latter. Courtyards separate women's space from men's space, private doors allow women to enter and leave the house discretely, and windows in the interior of the housing, facing familial areas, ensure privacy. The system of seclusion, or *hareem* (from where the word *harem* stems), extends into the house itself. Men often have a section of the home for greeting male friends that is separate from the family area of the house, where women move freely. This male front area is often called a *majlis* or *diwaniyah* and serves as a parlor room for visiting. Whether the house is a Bedouin tent or a large mansion, the *majlis* area is an important component of architecture as well as social life.

The Bedouin tent is structurally the simplest of Gulf dwellings. Because the desert environment was harsh and provided few building materials, the Bedouin turned to their animals for resources. Women wove the tents, known as *bayt shaar*, or "house of hair," from camel or goat hair, creating black panels that they knitted together into larger pieces. In the event of damage, women had the responsibility of mending and maintaining the panels; in some tribes, women set up the tents as well. Afterward, women embroidered the panels with stripes and other details using brightly colored wool that would be highly visible on the black background. Embroidery was limited to the sides of panels, but once they were joined, they created an allover bright and decorative pattern.

Although the tents were not large in comparison with modern houses, they were sufficient for a family to live in comfortably, especially if outdoor spaces and other tents (nondwelling) provided alternate living areas. There was a flexibility of space, with the same area offering different possibilities for usage. Tents were partitioned into at least two sections, effectively resulting in male and female areas, where family members could entertain visitors without encountering members of the opposite sex. Women also wove the *sahah*, or dividing wall, which was hung to demarcate space. As a weaving, the *sahah* had one good face, and that was the one that faced the men's side of the tent. Because the Bedouin had a nomadic lifestyle, their dwellings had to be flexible and functional. Tents were constructed to accommodate movement; they could be rolled up when the group needed to move. They also needed to provide protection from the hot sun and warmth during the cool winter nights. As there was not a lot of room for storage, possessions were kept to a minimum, and thus tents were not built with storage rooms. Today, most Bedouin are

Village ruins, al-Fujayrah Emirate. Courtesy of Anders Linde-Laursen.

settled in permanent dwellings, but the *bayt shaar* still enjoys great popularity and is iconic of Bedouin hospitality. During Ramadan and special occasions, hotels and families construct tents for receiving guests. Likewise, when young men and families take to the desert for weekends, they often reside in tents, albeit of man-made materials, recalling days of yore.

After the tent, the fundamental unit of architecture is the house, which can be quite modest or elaborate; available materials, social values, and the wealth of the resident, rather than architectural style, dictated the size and form of the residence. Most construction materials were taken from the surrounding landscape—palm trees, *sarooj* (mud mixed with hay and manure), *juss* (limestone mortar mix), and coral or gypsum shaped into building blocks. When cement became available in the 1950s, it supplanted many traditional construction materials as it required less preparatory work and could be used for multistory structures. Regardless of building material, houses were constructed to adapt to both the natural and social environments—ventilation systems offered cooling during hot summer months, and houses had *majlises*, courtyards, and private areas.

Date palm houses were quite common in the early years of city settlement as well as around oases. Made from all parts of the date palm, these houses, which are called *barasti* in English and *khayamah* (also the word for tent) or *'arishah* in Arabic, utilized available resources. Palm trunks provided support for the walls and beams of the house, while palm branches, stripped of leaves, were fastened together into mats that served as the walls of the house. Fronds, which were stripped from the branches, provided weaving material for thinner mats that were used as flooring, as insulation in wintertime, and, when bundled together, as the rooftop. Because the houses had natural gaps due to construction materials, they could benefit from breezes. There are variations on the *barasti* house based on location and available materials—rarely were they more than one story or built from many other materials beyond, for example, small boulders at their base or the incorporation of mud bricks. When needed, these houses were renewed and were considered permanent dwellings, as opposed to the Bedouin tent, which was fundamentally a portable home.

While poorer people built *barasti* houses, the wealthier built larger residences out of block and more permanent materials. These early houses were regular and rectangular in shape and were built around one or more inner courtyards, with one entrance for the family and another entrance for male visitors. Depending on the angle of the sun, shade would encompass different parts of the house's inner areas, providing places to work or gather at all hours of the day. Moreover, by constructing houses around central courtyards and with multiple entrances, occupants could maintain privacy for women as well as open doors to visitors. People sought other ways to ensure privacy as well. Perimeter walls were built high enough to ensure that occupants were not visible from the alleyways that snaked through settlements. Windows either were very small and faced the street or were located solely on the interior of the house toward the family courtyard. Thus women could move about freely within the house without risk of encountering men who were considered prohibited based on marriage conventions. Small windows also provided relief from the hot sun, helping the house's internal temperature remain bearable. Many houses had rooftop sleeping platforms, where family members could gain some respite from hot summer nights.

Houses were rarely more than one story tall for a number of reasons. Construction materials could not structurally support tall buildings, and if more room was needed to accommodate additional family members, people added rooms laterally, rather than building upward. Additionally, if all houses were similar in height, neighbors could not look down from upper areas into the private spaces of neighboring buildings. The only exceptions to this were sheikhs' houses, which stood out with two or more stories, preventing others from peering into their courtyards.

In a climate with very hot summers and, in coastal areas, extreme humidity, buildings relied on nonmechanized ventilation systems that both cooled and

Restored wind tower, Bastakiya neighborhood, Dubai, UAE. Courtesy of Elizabeth Faier.

circulated air. Materials such as date palm and coral are naturally porous and thus prevent the buildup of heat within the house during long summer days. Likewise, courtyards helped air circulate among rooms, venting hot air to the outside and allowing cooler air to enter inside. Two ventilation systems—the *barjeel*, or wind tower, and the *badqeer*, or wall wind puller system—captured and channeled air in unique ways. The elegant *barjeel* was a tower that rose above the house. Its sides were angled in such a way that they captured breezes, funneling the cool area into the house while, at the same time, providing an outlet for the release of warmer air. The tower opened into a room or area in the house. In summer, beds were kept in these areas as they were significantly cooler than other rooms, and during winter, the opening was closed to prevent warm air from leaving the house. The *badqeer* functioned in a similar manner, only instead of moving air through a tower, its ventilation system focused on the walls. As many houses did not have windows that faced the street, capturing breezes was a problem. With the *badqeer* system, two walls about five inches apart trapped breezes, pushing the cooler air through windows in the interior and letting warmer air escape through the gaps between the walls. In both cases, cooler air was brought into the house and warmer air was allowed to exit. As the Bedouin tent is iconic of nomadic Arab life, the wind tower stands out as a symbol of early city life before air-conditioning.

Although various factors determined the form of a structure, decorative elements were also employed for enhancement, many of which were borrowed from nearby areas. The wind tower was directly imported from Iran, while carved wood balconies, verandas, and doors reflected Indian influences. The Gulf region is not particularly forested, so wood is imported from India for thresholds, doors, shutters, and decorative details. Large, elaborate wooden balconies grace some older houses, standing out in relief against adobe-colored buildings. On low, barred windows, often to *majlis* areas, wooden internal shutters offer beauty and privacy. Similarly, *mushrabiyat*, or perforated plaster panels often adorned with repetitive patterns, cover other openings. *Naqsh* carvings, or carved panels, decorate portals and, when money and structure allow, punctuate crevices. These carvings are naturalistic in design and feature repetitive geometric patterns that evoke a wallpaper or trellis feel. In large buildings, shaped corner reinforcements stand along the roofline, recalling the fortification of corners found in fortresses. Not only do these details articulate the shape of the rooftop, but also they prevent the possibility of evil spirits (djinn) from settling. Locks historically were secured to the outside of buildings. Often carved from wood or forged from iron, they added another layer of adornment.[1]

Public Buildings

Each community had a number of public buildings constructed out of more durable materials. *Suq*s were the hallmark of trading communities, allowing goods to move in and out of waterfronts and providing locals with shopping areas. In both residential and commercial areas, mosques afforded people places to pray as well as to meet for Friday sermons. Mosques also doubled as schools or had separate schools attached to them. There, male children would learn the Quran and basic subjects such as reading, writing, and arithmetic. Fortresses, often located in the middle of cities, and watchtowers on the edges of communities served as residences for sheikhs and provided safety during wars. Public buildings were the bedrock of the community, providing places for commerce, education, religion, governance, and defense as well as opportunities for social interaction.

*Suq*s were usually located near waterfront areas for ease of trade. They brought traders together to offer their goods and were often organized into specialized markets, offering buyers items such as gold, animals, and spices. Today, the layout of the traditional *suq* is not always evident given how modern Gulf cities have developed. For example, in Manama, the *suq* today sits

Spice *suq*, Dubai, UAE. Courtesy of Anders Linde-Laursen.

away from the water because land reclamation efforts have extended building into what was once the harbor area. In Doha, there is the concentrated
effort to reconstruct the traditional *suq*s in ways that reflect original planning
and functions. Traditional markets continue to function in Muscat, winding
from the corniche through neighborhood streets. In general, a main street or
alleyway comprised the central area of the *suq*, off which, if the *suq* was large,
winding passageways would extend. At each end of the primary street stood a
gate that would be closed at sunset when the *suq* closed, clearly demarcating
the space. The roofline of the *suq* was usually quite high, many meters tall, and
covered with palm frond mats, allowing for shade as well as the rising of hot
air. In some *suq*s, later additions included the installation of more permanent
roofs and wind towers. Alongside the street, merchants erected small rooms,
or stores, from coral or gypsum blocks, providing individual outlets for each
trader.

Defensive buildings served two purposes: they were homes of tribal leaders,
and they provided the community with shelter during times of conflict. The
remains of forts today bear witness to their large scale, an architectural achieve-
ment given local materials and building techniques. Fortresses are imposing
structures with large, thick walls (often two feet thick), fortified entrances, a

Al-Jalali Fort (renovated by Portugese in 1500s) next to Sultan Qaboos' Palace, Muscat, Oman. Courtesy of Anders Linde-Laursen.

few small external windows, two or more stories in height, numerous rooms and courtyards, and round or square watchtowers rising above the main structure. Constructed out of the most durable materials possible, they were fortified against small arms and not built for very long siege periods. In Oman, the legacy of Portuguese occupation is especially evident; flanking the Sultan's palace are the Jalali and Mirani forts, which were constructed on the site of earlier Omani forts but heavily renovated by the Portuguese.

Mosques reflect a variety of forms and styles, from the grand mosque structures in places like Oman and the UAE to the single-room, simple mosques that are the norm in Qatar. The tower, or *burj*, from where the call to prayer was announced varies dramatically in shape and size. Some mosques have relatively low towers with domed tops, while others have towering minarets. It is unclear whether the variation arises from regional differences or from religious beliefs. For example, the minimal towers on early Qatari mosques could be due to Wahabist influences that reject ostentation. Likewise, Omani mosques tend to have smaller, domed minarets, painted in shades of blue and green, which differ from the more angular and intricate minarets of much of the Gulf. In Oman's interior regions, the mosques are simple, reflecting the austere aesthetic of Ibadism. Today's mosques have taller minarets than earlier mosques, perhaps in response to changing architectural styles or the need to reach larger areas than in previous generations.[2] In addition to local mosques,

Community mosque outside Muscat, Oman. Courtesy of Elizabeth Faier.

cities have grand mosques that are built by ruling families. In Abu Dhabi, the Sheikh Zayed Grand Mosque can accommodate thirty thousand people and boasts fifty-seven domes and four minarets, giving it grandeur unlike any other mosque in the UAE and standing out as one of the largest mosques in the world. Similarly, Muscat's Sultan Qaboos Grand Mosque, which provides tours for non-Muslims, serves as a religious center as well as housing a research library. With thirty-five crystal chandeliers, an expansive prayer carpet (over 275 feet), and other ornamentation, this large mosque exhibits an example of lavish Islamic architecture.

Contemporary Architecture

While the architectural style of contemporary buildings is varied, many recall the past social and economic life in the Gulf with their imagery, shape, and decoration. Buildings can evoke the new and unusual, incorporate traditional motifs such as repeating arches, or pattern themselves after real-life objects such as a ship. It is not uncommon to see a building with many different architectural elements or built in unusual shapes such as round or triangular structures. Omani architecture differs most from the rest of the Gulf, reflecting its varied topography (and thus resources and traditions) as well as other influences, especially the Indian Mogul architectural style. Today's housing shares some similarities with traditional dwellings, especially the segregation of social spaces and the incorporation of courtyard or outside areas within the house structure.

Contemporary dwellings include large and small houses, apartment complexes, and, more recently, furnished hotel apartments. Most locals prefer houses and only live in apartments out of financial necessity or ease if they maintain multiple residences. Unlike early houses, which were modest and utilitarian, many of today's homes, especially in the wealthier Gulf states of Qatar and the UAE, are veritable mansions, with multiple entrances; elaborate and unique ornamentation; numerous bedrooms; multiple *majlis* spaces; and large, green gardens. It is not unheard of for a house to have upward of nine bedrooms as well as separate quarters for domestic workers such as maids and drivers. While high walls surround these houses to ensure privacy, they also have large windows and balconies facing the outside. Some Bedouin construct outdoor *majlis* areas in cooler months, pitching a tent on a poured concrete platform that lies near the front of the house.

Construction usually employs concrete block and cement mortar as these are readily available and allow for more varied structures than past materials. For taller buildings, steelwork is also used. House facades can be made from a variety of materials, including marble, tile, gypsum, and high-tech materials. Many residential and public buildings sport wide expanses of windows or even entire walls of glass. Multipaned, insulated, and tinted glass windows minimize heat buildup and noise from traffic. Nationals primarily control the construction industry, employing laborers from south Asia (India, Pakistan, Sri Lanka, Nepal) and, more recently, China. In general, the industry is fraught with problems, especially in Qatar and the UAE, where recent accidents have raised concerns over laborer safety and general safety guidelines.

All major Gulf cities have landmark buildings. Kuwait Towers, two large minaret-shaped buildings with a revolving restaurant and observation platforms, light up the sky of Kuwait City. In Doha, the West Bay development features numerous modern skyscrapers and unique architectural buildings such as the triangular-shaped Sheraton hotel. Downtown Doha features the Islamic Cultural Center, with its spiraling facade. Contrasting with Muscat's low, whitewashed buildings are grand hotel developments, including the Bustan Palace, which features gardens; a high, domed interior laden with gold; and numerous interior archways. Although still being built, Manama will soon feature a waterfront of futuristic, glass-and-steel skyscrapers that spiral into the sky and curve along the ground. Abu Dhabi, often referred to as the Manhattan of the Gulf, with its grid layout, towering buildings, wide sidewalks, and compact island layout, is home to the majestic Emirates Palace. The full-service hotel sits along the corniche, features separate wings and entrances for visiting royalty, and showcases an interior of gilded tiles, chandeliers, and oriental carpets. Although it cannot be confirmed, rumor was that the gold market fluctuated when gold inlay was applied to its ornate interior. Dubai, though, is perhaps best known as an architectural showcase, striving to have over one hundred unique architectural towers, including the Burj al-Dubai, which, when complete (in fall 2009), will be the tallest building in the world. Other famous landmarks include the Burj al-Arab, considered locally to be a wonder of the world; the Gate, a massive, squared archway; the World Trade Center, with its tower of archway-covered floors; and numerous other buildings that line Sheikh Zayed Road and the Dubai Creek.

These architectural wonders not only reflect the concentration of wealth in the Gulf, but also raise questions about whether a new regional architectural style is developing. Residents often speak out about their concerns that Gulf development will embrace a global style of architecture, a style that replicates international standards and does not reflect the cultural or historical

Kuwait Towers. Courtesy of Dave Hutton.

traditions of a place. For example, the Dubai Cultural Council has been surveying locals and expatriates about their understanding of the character of the city, concerned that with its new projects, Dubai no longer speaks to its origins. Likewise, in Doha, people associate new development and construction with Western problems, suggesting that modern urban planning can be linked with Western forms of domination. However, studies in Kuwait (Andersen and al-Bader 2006) suggest that increasingly, a new form of architectural style that embraces and transforms heritage is emerging. This regional style utilizes traditional motifs and shapes as well as colors to evoke the sea, sky, and desert.

MATERIAL CULTURE

Islam prohibits the literal depiction of human and animal forms, and thus, in traditional art and decoration, one finds geometric designs, calligraphy, and other decorative motifs. In general, the prohibition stems from the belief that only God, or Allah, is a creative force, and to depict humans is to mimic the power of God in creation. While one does find photographs and paintings, especially of ruling families, much of the Gulf's material culture is limited to utility items such as jewelry, household items, and building decoration, or arts that reflect cultural and religious traditions such as calligraphy and weaving. Common motifs draw from everyday life, including the coffeepot, plants, flowers, and animals. Geometric designs in an arabesque style, or one that favors flowers, stars, and repetitive shapes, are found on everything from etched glasswork to housing gates. The arabesque style favors a pattern that splits with regularity and then reintegrates the shapes. For example, a house gate might have a series of stars that unfold into triangles and then merge again into stars. Usually, symmetry is favored as it creates a rhythm to the repetition and emphasizes the geometry of the design. However, folk beliefs also suggest that symmetry should be avoided as it seeks to replicate the perfection that only God, or Allah, could create. Thus it is common to find in carpets and on chests one or two elements that disrupt the symmetry of the overall pattern. It is also believed that integrating an imperfection into a design wards off evil spirits.

The textile art of weaving is found throughout the Gulf and is usually associated with Bedouin. Women were the weavers among the Bedouin, producing textiles for nearly all material daily needs: tents, dividing walls, camel bags, carpets, and storage bags. The looms were very basic and only allowed for simplistic designs such as stripes, chevrons, and other linear patterns. While geometric designs are most common, sometimes a representation of a common object is also woven into the fabric. Even on simple pieces, it is common to find a more elaborate border. Materials included both camel and

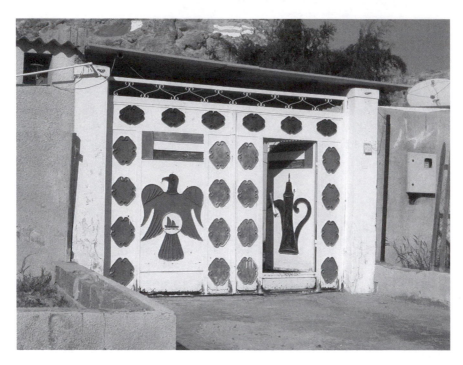

House gate with falcon, dhow, coffeepot, and flag symbols, Hatta, Dubai Emirate, UAE. Courtesy of Elizabeth Faier.

goat hair and, in some communities, cotton. Despite the availability of synthetic dyes, weavers favored natural dyes, which were laborious to produce. Pigment was extracted from different roots, barks, and leaves through pounding the materials, grinding them into a pulp, and then boiling them in dye vats. The basic looms could not accommodate large cloths. Thus smaller pieces were joined together, which also resulted in more complex patterns. When a weaving was complete, the ends were finished by braiding and, in the case of single-face weavings (many weavings could be used on either side), decorative tassels or other adornments might be added. *Al-sadu* is a form of folk art weaving, made from sheep wool, found in Kuwait and Qatar. Its brightly colored patterns adorn pillows, cushions, and saddlebags. In addition to woolen items, baskets were woven out of palm leaves; Karbabad in Bahrain is known for this art. Likewise, in many places, floor mats were woven out of sea grasses.

Dhow (traditional boat) building also combines utility and beauty. Dhows were traditionally used to ferry goods throughout the Gulf and today are primarily used for fishing. Previously powered by large sails, most dhows now rely on petrol engines, although, in competitions, people race traditional dhows

Large traditional dhow under construction, Dubai dhow yard on the Creek, Dubai, UAE. Courtesy of Elizabeth Faier.

with sails. The UAE is the center for the dhow-building industry, with buyers coming from all over the Gulf region. Master builders construct dhows according to traditional designs and by hand. A small boat can take approximately three months to complete, while larger boats can require many more months of labor. The building begins with the keel, after which the outside planking is finished and the ribs fitted into it; in the West, planking is fitted after a rib skeleton is constructed. There is the folk belief that says a woman can be ensured a male child if she jumps over the keel. However, the belief continues that the djinn will take a life for the life granted. Thus, during this early period of boat building, the master builder is especially nervous, working to complete the job as soon as possible and, in some cases, building fences to keep women out. Teak is the wood of choice, but increasingly, it is becoming too expensive for much beyond the hull. Metal nails are used to fasten the planks, and an ointment of boiled oil and animal fat is applied to increase its seaworthiness, prevent barnacles from attaching, and protect against woodworms. Finally, the dhow is finished with carvings and paintings (Gillespie 2006, 43–45).

Another commonly found folk art is calligraphy, the art of handwriting. In calligraphy, elaborate flourishes transform letters and words into intricate designs or pictures of objects. For example, a calligrapher might pen a folk saying in such a way that the words come together to form an image of an old man. Usually, though, calligraphic forms of writing are beautiful swirls of words that form interesting designs. Because the letters are extended, curled, and overlapped onto each other, calligraphy can be very difficult to read. Still, many common sayings and Quranic verses are often written so that they are easily recognizable by just a few words. In the case of Quranic verses, it is unacceptable to depict them in figurative form because the writing itself is considered to be God's words. Calligraphy is used to create jewelry, decorate buildings, and produce paintings for household decoration. The artists' elaborate designs reflect an Islamic aesthetics through the use of geometric shapes and the interweaving of patterns to produce light and dark areas. The proportion of each letter to the others is based on mathematical rules, and thus the calligrapher is a highly skilled and respected artist with years of training.

Artisanship and beauty are also appreciated in daily utilitarian items. Men's objects symbolize bravery and masculinity and adhere to Islamic rules governing bodily adornment. Islam prohibits men from wearing jewelry and gold, and thus material culture associated with males is utilitarian and crafted out of acceptable materials. Perhaps the best-known item is the *khanjar*, or curved dagger, which is commonly found in Oman, Qatar, and the UAE. The *khanjar* is a sharp knife with a handle crafted from bone or wood and polished to a smooth surface. Men wear the *khanjar* around the waist on a belt of leather and silver or fabric. Because of its location on the body, the *khanjar* is sheathed in a curved container that looks like a *J*. The sheath is an item of beauty, made from intricate silverwork. Often the silver threads would wind around the circumference, creating a relief surface of silver spirals and scrolls. The amount of decoration reflected the wealth of the owner. Originally worn on an everyday basis, today, the *khanjar* is primarily used on semiformal occasions.

Women adorn themselves with gold jewelry and clothing embroidered with gold thread (see Chapters 5 and 6 for further discussion of jewelry and clothing). Gold is valued throughout the Gulf because of its beauty, economic value, and role in weddings. Originally, jewelry was fashioned out of silver, but with greater wealth, gold became the favored material as its worth is higher. The gold favored in the Gulf is purer than that found in Western countries; it is common to find twenty-two-karat and twenty-four-karat gold, which is softer and has a very yellow hue. Heavy gold pieces and intricate, delicate items are favored, sparkling with bangles and other moving pieces that catch the light. Common items include *al-mirtaesha*, a gold necklace that covers the chest and extends to the waist; *al-tasa*, a head necklace that fits on the hair with a mesh of gold; and *al-kaff*, a bracelet

Gold shops in Kuwait City. Courtesy of Dave Hutton.

that covers much of the front of the hand. Today, yellow gold continues to be popular, but other prestige metals are also enjoyed, including platinum and white gold; diamonds and gemstones are also very popular, especially pavé patterns that use many small pieces to create the illusion of larger stones.

NOTES

1. See http://www.catnaps.org/islamic/gulfarch.html.
2. See http://www.catnaps.org/islamic/gulfarch.html.

5

Food, Dress, and Personal Adornment

THEIR VARIETY OF food and clothing reflect the myriad of cultures, traditions, and religions of the Arabian Gulf countries. It is customary to wear types of clothing and eat specific foods that are local to one's country or tribe. Consumption practices reflect individual tastes as well as signify publicly regional and ethnic identity. It is common to see south Asian women dressed in saris, Gulf women in *abayas* (black cloaks), and European women in Western-style clothing in shopping malls. Likewise, restaurants offer an array of eating choices such as American hamburgers, Chinese dim sum, Indian *biryanis*, and Lebanese kebabs.

While people often choose clothing and food that is familiar to them, the Arab Gulf states are multicultural environments where hybridization occurs in all facets of daily life. Eating foods that are not familiar or wearing ethnic clothing of a different group are not unusual, but rather, signifiers of personal taste. For example, a Qatari woman dressed in an *abaya* might be wearing jeans and a T-shirt underneath, or an Australian expatriate might be wearing Indian-styled clothing. Similarly, it is not unusual to see young Gulf men sporting baseball caps and Italian shoes with their dress-like garments, called *thoub*s. Western, Arab, and Asian foods and dress are found nearly everywhere: restaurants, grocery stores, and shopping malls. Still, most groups continue to associate the foods they eat and the clothes they wear with cultural and regional heritage.

FOOD AND EATING PRACTICES

Throughout the Gulf, people consider eating a meal and drinking coffee a social experience best shared with family members, close friends, and honored guests; this is especially true for local populations. People gather for barbeques in the desert, prepare elaborate meals with traditional foods, meet for Friday brunches, and relax at coffee shops watching soccer and smoking a *shisha* (water pipe). Regardless of the occasion, eating a meal with someone signifies a social relationship in which guests and hosts have specific roles and obligations to one another. Drinking coffee, whether in a *shisha* café or an international-style coffee shop such as Starbucks, also involves reciprocal social obligations, although to a lesser extent. Much of the social and business life of the Gulf revolves around eating with someone, offering opportunities for affirming relationships and for making new networks. While all nationalities spend large amounts of time sharing food and drink, the places they frequent and their customary practices differ according to background, class, and religion.

Daily Rhythms

Breakfast is a small meal, eaten at home early in the morning. Usually, bread, olives, yogurt, fried cheese (*halloumi*), and, in some countries, meat compose the meal, providing energy for the day's activities. Salty foods, such as *halloumi* and olives, also help people retain water and ward off the effects of dehydration that often occur in hot climates. Although some restaurants offer American and English breakfast menus that feature baked goods, eggs, breakfast meats, and baked beans, breakfast is not commonly eaten out of the house or on the go. The primary exception to the small meal occurs on Fridays, when people often gather for large buffet brunches that begin in the late morning. For expatriates, especially Westerners, Friday brunches are lively occasions that often involve alcohol and extend late into the afternoon.

Lunch or the midday meal is eaten usually around one or two o'clock in the afternoon and remains the most substantial meal of the day. It includes meat and rice dishes, cooked vegetables, salads, and bread. Workplace cafeterias, cafés, and restaurants are popular locales for eating lunch, although some people, if their schedules permit, prefer to return home and eat with their families. In earlier decades, especially before the advent of air-conditioning, going home in the middle of the afternoon was possible as businesses closed for the mid-afternoon hours and reopened later in the day, usually around 4:00 P.M. As the days are hottest during this time period, people could enjoy a meal and a bit of respite from the sun and heat. Today, some businesses continue to close during the mid-afternoon, but increasingly, businesses are operating on a Western business schedule.

The dinner meal varies dramatically and can range from a large meal with multiple courses to a light meal of salads, breads, and fruit. Locals tend to eat smaller dinner meals, unless celebrating a special occasion. Often, people will graze on light foods through the evening, in part because of the substantial midday meal. In every major city, cafeterias and restaurants offer dinner, usually starting after seven in the evening—very late night dining is uncommon. Diners in restaurants tend to be expatriates, although local populations also meet for a meal or coffee in the evening.

In the evenings after dinner, people visit each other, meet for coffee, or spend time in their homes. International-style coffeehouses are popular places for people to meet and are conveniently located in shopping malls. More traditional cafés attract men, often locals and Arabs, for an evening of smoking *shisha*, sharing conversation, and watching television. While these cafés generally do not prohibit women, it is uncommon for women to frequent them as they are considered male-only areas and thus inappropriate for women, especially women unaccompanied by men.

Food Shopping

Large supermarkets located within or adjacent to shopping malls are popular places for buying food and household necessities. These megashops sell an unimaginable variety of packaged foods, produce, meats, clothing, electronics, household items, and furniture to satisfy both European and Asian customers. Many countries ban the sale of pork and other products made from pigs as Islamic law prohibits pork. In countries where the sale of pork is permitted, special rooms in supermarkets offer pork products—these rooms are open only to non-Muslims. Supermarkets cater to different ethnic populations. For example, some stores are known for their south Asian products, vegetables, and meats, while others stock more British or American items. Correspondingly, while people may shop at any supermarket they choose, people often frequent those that sell familiar products.

In addition to large megamarkets, smaller supermarkets, grocers, and convenience stores dot many neighborhoods. In some countries, local coops sell a smaller variety of goods than the large supermarkets but serve national interests and thus tend to primarily serve local customers. Despite their size, small neighborhood shops stock an enormous variety of items, often with boxes and goods stacked to the ceiling and with aisles barely large enough for an individual to squeeze through. People rarely do their weekly shopping at these stores, but frequent them for forgotten or hard-to-find items. Because these neighborhood shops primarily serve residential communities, they offer delivery services.

Meat products are usually purchased at supermarkets, although when individuals want to slaughter their own animals, they might make a trip to the local abattoir, or slaughterhouse. Fish can be bought at supermarkets or at fish *suq*s, or markets, located near fisherman huts or in some neighborhoods. Fish markets sell fish from local waters as well as imported fresh items from nearby countries. These markets tend to open early in the morning and close their doors by late afternoon. It is wisest to visit them early as the selection is best and the odors less overwhelming. Unlike the supermarkets, bargaining is not only normal, but also expected.

Similarly, in the fruit and vegetable markets, bargaining is expected as sellers haggle with buyers to negotiate a satisfactory price. Once, fruit and vegetable markets were common destinations where people would go to buy fresh produce, often from regional producers. However, with the advent of large supermarkets with wider varieties of produce and long opening hours, they are quickly disappearing. In some countries, these *suq*s only serve the wholesale market or families who wish to buy in bulk.

Traditional Foods

Islamic law prohibits Muslims from eating pork or consuming alcohol. Moreover, Muslims are required to eat meat of animals that have been slaughtered according to Islamic ritual practice. Meat produced in this manner is called "halal," which means "permissible." In order for meat to be considered halal, the animal must be slaughtered according to *dhabiha* practices, which involve slicing through the major arteries in an animal's neck with a single cut. Islamic dietary laws are quite complicated and go beyond slaughtering to include a number of prohibitions, including blood and fish with scales. Although halal most often refers to meat, it widely refers to anything that is permissible according to Islamic law. The opposite of halal is *haram*, which means "forbidden" and, like the term *halal*, refers to a larger category than food items. People will often say "*haram*" to show disapproval or concern, rather than denote something that is not permissible for consumption.

Traditional dishes use the spices, fish, fruits, dairy products (mainly yogurt), and vegetables found in the region. Common flavorings include cardamom, turmeric, saffron, and dried limes. Before vegetables were widely available, the Gulf diet relied heavily on meat that came from their animals. Meat remains popular, especially lamb and mutton. Roasted meats served with fragrant and fruit-studded dishes are popular, with each country having a slight variation that reflects its roots and trade patterns. While there are variations, the dish *machbous* refers to a spiced meat and rice that is served communally. Often, an

entire roasted young camel or sheep is served on beds of rice for special occasions, with the different parts of the animal split among communal dishes. In
Kuwait, *khouzi*, or baked lamb stuffed with rice, is popular. In countries such
as Qatar and the United Arab Emirates (UAE), *hareis*, lamb slowly cooked
with wheat, is commonly served as a national dish. For Westerners, *hareis* is
something of an acquired taste as, after many hours of cooking, the meat and
wheat blend into each other, creating a soft paste. In Oman, a similar dish is
served. *Shuwa* is spiced meat that cooks very slowly in an underground clay
pot for up to two days, which makes it very tender. *Biryanis*, or fragrant rice,
fruit, and vegetable/meat dishes that come from south Asia, are not only very
popular, but also resemble traditional Gulf dishes; many Gulf dishes reflect a
south Asian influence.

In addition to traditional Gulf dishes, dishes from other parts of the
Arab world, especially Lebanon, are a staple of the local diet. *Wara enab* or
dolma, which are grape leaves stuffed with rice, herbs, and tomatoes, are commonly found on menus, as are mixed grills of meat, including *shish tawouk*
(grilled chicken on spits), *kofta* (grilled ground meat and parsley molded
around skewers), and *lamb kabobs*. *Shwarma*, grilled spiced meat sliced off
a rotisserie, is also popular as a sandwich or main dish. Likewise, falafel,
small, deep-fried balls of chickpeas that can be eaten stuffed into a sandwich
with fries, along with fresh and pickled vegetables, is popular. For breakfast,
some people favor *foul*, which is made from fava beans that are cooked in a
tomato broth and then topped with chopped vegetables, mainly tomatoes and
onions. Like *shwarma* and falafel, *foul* is considered an inexpensive and filling
meal.

Salads are very popular beginnings and accompaniments to meals.
Hummus, a mixture of mashed chickpeas, sesame paste (tahini), lemon juice,
and garlic, is served alongside bread. Tabbouleh, a salad of cracked wheat
(bulgur), parsley, tomatoes, and cucumbers, is often eaten as a salad, as is *fat-
toush*, a mixed vegetable salad spiced with sumac and topped with toasted
pita bread squares. Side dishes made from vegetables are a favorite for starters.
Roasted and mashed eggplant, or *moutabel*, which is similar to baba ghanoush,
is eaten, as is *bamia*, an okra dish cooked with lamb in a tomato sauce.

Many of these salads comprise a staple of the meze, a collection of small
dishes that is commonly eaten as an afternoon meal. Meze is similar to the
Spanish tapas, as one orders or prepares a variety of dishes with small servings
to make a spread of hot and cold vegetable and meat offerings. Other popular
dishes in a meze (although some can also be eaten alone as a meal) include
koussa mahshi, or hollowed-out marrow (similar to small zucchinis) stuffed
with rice and ground meat, and *kibbi*, small pockets of cracked wheat stuffed
with ground meat and pine nuts and then deep fried. Stuffed dishes, such as

koussa mahshi, wara enab, and *kibbi*, require a great deal of labor to prepare, yet are very popular staples on restaurant and home menus.

Dairy dishes round out many menus. Yogurt takes many forms in the Gulf, providing tangy accompaniment for many dishes as well as an alternative to *tahini* for dipping. Some people like to start their day with a slightly sour drink called *laban*, which is made from yogurt and has the consistency of buttermilk. Dishes made from yogurt, cucumbers, mint, and other herbs provide refreshment and complement the taste of meat and rice dishes as well as meze samplings. Yogurt cheese, or *labneh*, is also popular and is made at home or bought from markets. Draining away the excess water from yogurt over a period of many hours results in a soft cheese with a consistency similar to cream cheese. *Labneh* is then formed into balls and stored in oil or spread onto bread and eaten as a sandwich. Yogurt's popularity stems from its versatility: yogurt products spoil less frequently than those made directly from cow's milk. Valued for its health benefits, camel milk is a popular drink, although certainly an acquired taste for foreigners, who often note its pungent qualities. With less fat and sugar than cow milk, camel milk is considered a health drink aiding everything from diabetic to vascular problems. Readily available in supermarkets, camel milk can be purchased in the dairy aisle.

Another staple item on the Gulf menu is bread. Pita, small, flat pockets of wheat bread, makes its way into nearly all meals—whole as a sandwich casing, sliced as a dipping item for hummus, and cut into wedges as a side dish. *Manaqeesh*, which is similar to a pita pizza, is very popular as a morning or early afternoon dish. Made from pita dough that is topped with meats, eggs, cheese, and vegetables and then baked in a clay oven, *manaqeesh* varieties are endless. Popular flavors include egg and cheese; *zaatar* (an herb mix similar to oregano), oil, and sesame seed; and red pepper slices. Large flat breads are also enjoyed, usually baked on top of a hot drum so they end up crispy sheets ready for spreading with *labneh* or *zaatar*, to be rolled into a filling sandwich. *Sambousas*, triangular, deep-fried pastries that are stuffed with vegetables or meat, are commonly found in bakeries, but their origins lie in south Asia.

Every meal concludes—and sometimes begins—with sweets, which are an important part of the diet. *Umm ali* is one of the most popular desserts found in nearly all Gulf countries. Something of a cross between a bread pudding and pudding, *umm ali* is a very sweet, fragrant custard made from baked pita pieces, milk, raisins, and nuts. Other custard-like dishes from the Gulf also complete meals, such as *mehalabiya*, made with rosewater and pistachios, and *muhammar*, made from brown rice and sugar or dates. Numerous types of pastries made from layers of flaky, buttery sheets of filo dough, nuts, rosewater, and sugar are also found but originate from other Arab countries such as

Lebanon. These baklava varieties are sold in specialty stores and are featured on every Arab menu.

A few other forms of sweet items make up the heritage of the Gulf region. *Halwa*, in Oman, symbolic of hospitality, is served to guests during religious and other important occasions and in times of happiness and sorrow. Skilled *halwa* makers prepare the dessert from starch, eggs, sugar, nuts, and spices such as cardamom. Once finished, *halwa* can be kept for months without refrigeration. Essentially a sticky paste, *halwa* might not look very appealing, but many praise its sweet and tasty qualities. Also in Oman, one can find a form of whipped sugar that is similar to cotton candy but flavored with sesame and pistachio. Another local specialty found in Oman as well as other Gulf states is *lokhemat*. Often served as an accompaniment to coffee, *lokhemat* are deep-fried dumplings flavored with cardamom and served with sweet syrup. A favorite with any meal, *lokhemat* can also be commonly found at heritage displays, where older women sit around pots of hot oil, frying up balls for onlookers, who eagerly await the treat.

Traditionally, dates play a central part in Gulf cuisine as symbols of hospitality and nurturance. Date palms are found throughout the region, especially in oases where they are farmed as a local and export product. Raw dates are often eaten during the fall months and, unlike their dried counterparts, are hard and bitter to the taste. Dried dates can be prepared in numerous ways, resulting in dates with distinct tastes, from the very sweet and juicy to the fleshy and savory. It is also common to split dates, remove the stone, and stuff them with dried orange peel, blanched almonds, or other items that complement the sweet and chewy quality of the dried fruit. Specialty stores that sell date varieties as well as date drinks abound, packaging date collections as one would fine chocolates. Dates are almost always offered to guests as locals take pride in their richness and variety. Many other fruits are eaten, a number of which are tropical fruits from south Asia. Popular fruits include the rambutan, a small, hairy, reddish fruit that tastes a bit like a lychee, and mangosteen, a purple fruit with segments that have a sweet-tart flavor.

Dining

Nationals honor guests and mark holiday occasions, such as the Iftars or evening meals during Ramadan, with a meal that unfolds according to customary practices of hospitality and the eating of traditional foods. During Ramadan, it is customary to first break the fast with dried dates and a cool drink. It is said that the Prophet Muhammed broke his fast with dates, which provide a quick burst of sugar and give strength. After the fast is broken, people might eat a regular meal with meat, but usually with extra calories to offset the deficit from fasting, or attend a lavish Iftar buffet with a variety of traditional foods. Religious leaders and health officials encourage people to eat as they normally do, rather than gorge themselves on large, heavy meals with caffeine and sugar. People can continue eating, if they wish, up until the next morning, when the fast begins again. Often, a small meal that is similar to breakfast is eaten in the morning hours. Iftar buffets in restaurants are popular with both nationals and expatriates, who sometimes fast alongside Muslims.

In earlier periods, before the advent of oil wealth in the Gulf, it was customary for locals, especially Bedouin, to sit on the floor, eating without plates or cutlery from communal dishes. Today, most people do not eat around low tables or mats laid on the floor, except during holiday meals, when people want to connect with their tribal heritage and customary practice. Most homes have dining tables for everyday use. Serving family-style, sometimes from large metal trays, remains common for everyday and ritual meals. When eating from a communal platter, one uses the right hand to pull off meat or scoop food with bread because the left hand is associated with toilet hygiene and is thus considered dirty and contaminating. Everyday, however, people use dishes and flatware; for fine meals, china and silver might be used.

It is uncommon for a non-family-member or close friend to attend a casual meal, although sometimes people will host acquaintances at a restaurant or in the home during holidays. Guests are neither expected to bring a gift nor to contribute food dishes. Moreover, there are specific rules of hospitality to which both guests and hosts subscribe. For example, it is considered rude throughout the Gulf to show the soles of the feet, and thus people cross their legs accordingly. Likewise, guests are expected to accept a host's offering of food and drink. It is something of a myth that guests are expected to eat and drink everything given to them when visiting someone's house for a formal meal. However, guests should graciously partake in the host's hospitality. The amounts of food and drink laid before guests are usually more than one could actually consume, as excess is seen as a sign of honor and hospitality (see Chapter 7, on hospitality).

Going Out

Going to a coffeehouse to drink coffee or tea, read a paper, and talk with friends is a pastime in which nearly all people partake. Beyond that, coffeehouses vary drastically from international chains, such as Starbucks and Caribou Coffee, to local, all-male lounges where women are not banned but rarely frequent, as these spaces are considered no-go for women. Most malls and many neighborhoods have European-style coffeehouses that serve specialty drinks, pastries, and light meals. With comfortable furniture, newspapers, and opportunity for people watching, these cafés attract all kinds of clientele and provide safe, culturally acceptable environments for women to gather. Arab *shisha* coffeehouses are strictly male-only affairs where groups of men gather, talking the night away while puffing on water pipes. For women, primarily expatriates, who wish to smoke *shisha*, restaurants with cafés offer an alternative, as they are mixed-sex environments.

Driving a four-wheel-drive car into the desert for an evening of barbequing and star watching is a common weekend and holiday excursion. For those not lucky enough to have a four-wheel-drive vehicle or for those in search of a little more elegance than beach chairs and roaring coals, hotels offer barbeques at permanent desert campsites and at poolside areas, often with Bedouin-styled tents, cushions, and *shisha* pipes. To barbeque means more than simply stoking the fire. For locals, it is a way to connect with Bedouin life and enjoy the quiet of the desert and being with family. For expatriates and tourists, an evening barbeque features traditional grilled meats and fresh salads and, if on a tour, an evening of drumming and hair dance performances.

In most cities, hotels, private social clubs, and country clubs provide nightlife for the expatriate population; often, alcohol licenses are limited to these venues. Bars and clubs hold so-called quiz nights, where customers compete for prizes with their knowledge of trivia. Dance clubs offer specialty nights, from house scenes to salsa nights. The nightlife scene is especially vibrant in the UAE and Qatar, although Oman also offers a limited number of clubs.

CLOTHING AND DRESS STYLES

According to Islam, both men and women should dress modestly, exposing little bare skin to public gaze and wearing loose clothing that does not trace the figure. For women, this means loose dresses, long skirts, pants, and tunic-length blouses with long sleeves and some sort of veiling, or *hijab*, to cover the neck, shoulders, and hair. For men, clothing choices usually include Western pants, shirts, and suits or local dress, which tends to be long-sleeved, floor-length shirt-dresses; men from Southeast Asia often wear tunics and loose pants in light colors. Men also cover their heads with turbans, skullcaps, head-dresses, and baseball caps. Although not expected to wear national dress, expatriates are also expected to dress modestly and, despite the region's warm temperatures, not wear beach attire (shorts, sleeveless tops) on the streets. However, given the cosmopolitan environment of many Gulf states, many expatriates don dress that does not subscribe to Islamic codes of modesty. The tension between covering up and exposing the body as well as how different ethnic groups consider dressing in public fuels many debates in the newspapers concerning appropriate attire.

Popular images of Arab Gulf costume depict a homogenous sea of women covered in black robes from head to toe and men dressed in white robes and checkered or white head scarves. Locals take pride in wearing what is considered "national dress" in public, and while national dress does associate black clothing with women and white clothing with men, contemporary dress and folk costumes vary widely according to nation-state, settlement (rural vs. urban), region, age, contemporary fashion, and personal choice. In the same family, it is possible to find a young woman wearing a custom-designed scarf with Christian Dior logos and an older woman in a traditional face mask, or *burqa*. Likewise, in a shopping mall, one can see young Omani men dressed in lavender robes mingling with Saudi men dressed in white robes with cuff links and shirt collars. Omani dress differs the most, with coastal populations wearing clothing that looks most like other areas of the Gulf and inland groups wearing more colorful and regionally specific items.

Women's Clothing

Despite images of women clad in black robes, black scarves, and black facial masks, women's clothing in most of the Gulf states is quite colorful and diverse. In Kuwait and Bahrain, most women wear modestly styled Western clothing, often with a longer top or jacket over a skirt or slacks. Even the black outer robe, or *abaya*, that is associated with female Gulf dress varies widely in style and adornment, depending on individual taste and local tradition. For example, women in Dubai wear lavishly decorated *abayas* with embroidery, crystals, and other appliqués, while women in Qatar opt for a modestly adorned *abaya* with simple or no embroidery, although increasingly, Qatari *abayas* are also highly decorated items of clothing, especially when worn for special occasions. Oman is a different story, as women's dress reflects tribal associations, settlement, and traditions that draw from India, eastern Africa, and Yemen. Bright dresses are not uncommon, and women often wear the *burqa*. Most women wear clothing in public that is in some manner associated with Islamic and local codes of modesty: women cover their hair and wear loose-fitting clothes that obscure a woman's shape.

The *abaya* is a black outer garment favored in many parts of the Gulf. *Abayas* are always long-sleeved, full-length gowns that often trail on the ground and resemble, to a limited extent, a Western graduation gown. For many people in the West, the *abaya* symbolizes the cloistering or hiding away of females. To a large extent, the *abaya* has become emblematic for the West of women in the Gulf. However, this interpretation of the *abaya* differs radically from how most Gulf state locals perceive this item of clothing. Throughout the Gulf,

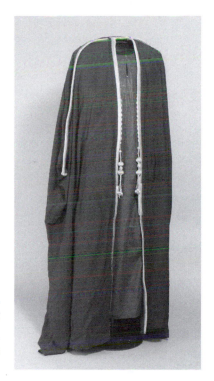

Pre-1959 *abaya* with embroidery and tassels from Qatar from the collection of Ferdinand Klaus at the Moesgaard Museum in Denmark. Courtesy of Richard Harris Photography.

locals associate the *abaya* with national dress and thereby wear it as part of a national costume. It is important to note that the *abaya* is not compulsory by law, as in Saudi Arabia, but a matter of choice, reflecting socially normative behavior. However, the *abaya* is a relatively new addition. In the early years of state formation, especially in the 1970s, many women did not wear the *abaya* as it was associated with older and traditional forms of wraps that women used to cover themselves when leaving the house. Gradually, though, the *abaya* has been adopted as the trademark of local dress, with many women noting that when they travel abroad, they do not wear the *abaya* because they are not in the home country. Although women have the choice to wear the *abaya* or not, there is strong social pressure to wear it, especially for married women and those over fourteen years old. At home or in family situations, women often do not wear the *abaya* as it seen as a garment to wear outside of the home.

The *abaya* comes in a myriad of styles, each uniquely tailored to the buyer's taste and physique. For many women, individuality in fashion is important, and they do not want to buy an *abaya* off the rack. Usually, the *abaya* is black, but some women opt for brightly colored *abayas*, which draw much attention.

In most areas, the *abaya* is a full-body cloak that reaches the ground, features long sleeves, and fastens in different manners. But that is where the commonalities end, as the cut, style, fasteners, material, and adornment choices are only limited by the buyer's or shopkeeper's imagination. Some *abayas* have zippered fronts, buttons, or hook and eye closures, while others are seamless and pulled over the head with or without a hood that also covers the hair. Cuts range from the currently popular butterfly, which features narrow arms and wide sleeves, to something more akin to a robe with wide arms and loose drape. Women seek out the latest designs from *abaya* fashion houses that not only offer different cuts, but also embellishments that range from tucks, pleats, and folds to kimono styling.

The array of choices continues, as buyers must select fabric, detailing, and length according to personal preference and usage. For example, women will hem their *abayas* according to the shoes they want to wear with a particular outfit. If the *abaya* is too long, women risk tearing the robe or, worse yet, tripping and harming themselves. If the *abaya* is too short, their feet will not be covered when walking or praying. Social practice dictates that the *abaya* must cover women's feet, whether standing up or in the prostrate position used for praying. Often, women will buy everyday *abayas* in silk crepe or other fabrics that provide some stretch, just in case they catch a sleeve or hem; *abayas* are also forgiving if women gain weight or become pregnant.

Although *abayas* are fundamentally modest garments, with the main purpose of averting attention from a woman's shape, they are sometimes revealing garments because of cut or transparency. Older women tend to favor more conservative versions with heavier materials, modest necklines, and little, if any, decoration. Younger generations prefer lighter garments with varying degrees of transparency that range from an *abaya* with sheer stripes to one that veils the clothing worn underneath. For parties and formal events, women of all ages prefer sheer materials, often silk, with fancy details, such as trailing hems, stitch work, velvet, or contrasting materials, and decoration such as crystals or embroidery. Women remark that while *abayas* are theoretically conservative clothing that should hide a women's shape and not be noticed, their variation and increasing ornamentation call attention to the wearer. Some conservative and religious women also wear socks and gloves along with their *abayas* and thus show little skin, even if their *abaya* flaps open or their sleeves draw upward in daily activities.

Because of the fashion industry surrounding the production and individualization of *abayas*, they are big business. Everyday *abayas* cost between two hundred and four hundred dollars, while evening *abayas*, which are worn to all-female events, cost from eight hundred dollars upward. Moreover, to protect the uniqueness and thus value of their garments, women are quite secretive about who made their outfits or where they shopped for the design, often sharing the name of tailors and merchants only with close friends and family. The number of *abayas* in a woman's closet also varies depending on income, social life, and need. Today, most women have at least ten *abayas*, although some have many more, and thus their wardrobes amount to sizeable investments. To care for these investments, women launder *abayas* with special washing powder that preserves their blackness and the life of the fine materials used in their construction.

Under the *abaya*, women wear either Western clothing, such as tops with pants or long skirts, or a loose caftan called a *jalabiya* (or *galabiya* in some dialects), which completely covers the arms and legs. The *jalabiya*, which is often favored by older women and considered traditional clothing, takes a number of forms. Traditionally, *jalabiyas* are two-piece dresses called a *thoub* and *kundra*, although they can be a one-piece dress as well. Although casual *jalabiyas* are made out of cotton and are considered to be housedresses, *jalabiyas* can also be elaborately decorated evening gowns made from silk organza and other luxurious fabrics costing thousands of dollars. Women often choose to wear *jalabiyas* when they are pregnant as the cut of the dress allows for a woman's changing size. *Jalabiyas* are also worn at formal and ritual events. During Ramadan, women favor the *jalabiya* for its comfort and beauty, as the Ramadan schedule often includes a large amount of visiting and eating.

A woman's choice of clothing reflects personal preference as well as her family's religious or social values, yet younger women are gradually opting for Western clothing. Gulf shopping malls offer the latest designers and styles, and great emphasis is placed on trendy and fashionable clothing. For wealthier women, the emphasis is on designer labels from European, Middle Eastern, and Indian fashion houses that offer high street fashion and the latest couture. Women also visit tailors to copy items found in fashion magazines, allowing for a cost-effective solution to expensive fashion items. In addition to seeking out the latest in Western styles, women place great emphasis on accessories, especially handbags, shoes, and trinket chains to hang on purses, mobile phones, and computer bags. Many companies release specialty accessories directed at the Gulf market such as jewel-encrusted phones.

The Veil

The *hijab*, or head covering, is considered an important part of Islamic dress, as hair is seen as a sexually enticing part of the body. Increasingly, women are wearing brightly colored or adorned *hijabs* that are specially made or fashioned from scarves. In the Gulf, the *hijab* is often referred to as a *shayla*, which is often a long piece of black silk crepe. Often made of the same black material used to create the *abaya,* the *shayla* is a long piece of fabric that can be placed over the top of the head with one side shorter than the other and then wound around the head a number of times to cover the hair and neck of the wearer. Women practice a number of tricks in securing the *shayla.* Some women place tiny pieces of Velcro to keep the *shayla* in place after it has been wound. Younger women often wear large hair clips around high ponytails that act as a peg for draping the *shayla.* While these hair clips help the *shayla* stay in place, they also enhance the silhouette of the woman's head, making it appear as if she has very long hair, which is seen as attractive. Despite how they are fastened, *shaylas* slip a lot in part because of the silky fabric from which they are fabricated. Consequently, women spend a lot of time winding and rewinding, pulling and pushing, folding and adjusting their *shaylas.*

While many women wear plain *shaylas* or *shaylas* made of fancy fabrics but without decoration, in recent years, great emphasis has been placed on creating a fashion design that links the *shayla* with the *abaya.* For example, if a woman opts for peacock feather embroidery on her *abaya,* she will carry over some of the same handiwork to her *shayla,* thereby creating a matched ensemble. Women also buy designer *shaylas* made by fashion houses such as Christian Dior. Often, they will buy a scarf with designer logos and then use it to trim the *abaya.* With the *shayla,* women express their uniqueness and individuality even more so than with the *abaya,* in part because they require less financial investment (although they often cost more than one hundred dollars apiece). A woman might dress up a plain *abaya* with a wildly colored *shayla* decorated with crystals, beads, and other appliqués. Likewise, many women style themselves by wearing only nonblack *shaylas,* perhaps because it is more acceptable for *shayla* colors to vary from black, particularly among young women.

Although the *shayla* is a form of veil in that it covers the hair, women in the Gulf employ other types of veils that cover the face as well. Thus, when speaking of veiling, most people refer to facial veils, rather than those that cover the hair. Two of the most common types of facial veils are the *niqab* and the *burqa;* the latter differs significantly from the veil in Afghanistan that shares its name. The *niqab* covers the face completely, except for the eyes, which are visible through a slit in the cloth or through a thin layer of gauze that fills the opening for the eyes. Religious and conservative women wear the *niqab,* which is always black and unadorned, as they interpret Islamic codes of veiling to include the *niqab.* Although it is worn with the *shayla,* the *niqab* is a separate piece of fabric that either ties around the head over the face or fits over the head on top of the *shayla.* Women who veil with the *niqab* wear it in public places, especially in areas where they might encounter men. Businesses or services that rely on facial recognition, such as banks and airports, usually accommodate women who wear the *niqab* by providing a private area where the veiled woman can show her face to a female officer.

Whether to wear the *niqab* is a hotly contested question in the Gulf. Some institutions refuse to hire women who wear the *niqab*, arguing that Islam does not prescribe such extensive veiling and that fully veiled women reinforce negative stereotypes of the Middle East. Women are allowed to drive with the *niqab*, but increasingly, this practice is questioned because officers cannot match the driver with the photograph on the driving license. Some Gulf locals find the *niqab* to be synonymous with tradition, while others suggest that the *niqab* is a backward but modern invention.

In contrast with the *niqab*, which is seen as a conservative garment worn by younger and older women, the *burqa* is associated more with tradition. It is usually worn by older women, Bedouin, and women who live in interior regions, especially in the UAE and Oman. *Burqas* can be substantial or minimal in their covering—some sit on the face as a mask, while others are worn over the head like a hood. Its shape varies widely, but there are a number of shared characteristics: slits for the eyes (covering the eyebrows); a stiff, protruding area over the nose that supports the mask; and some material to cover the mouth. The latter section over the mouth can be long, as favored by older women, or shorter, with space cut out so the lower lip is evident. *Burqas* can be fashioned from a number of different materials but are usually made from leather or indigo-stained cloth. Often, the material is treated so it has a shiny metallic sheen with golden hues; *burqas* can be decorated or left plain, but they always have sheen. Although *burqas* cover the face, they are generally considered to be an element of adornment that highlights a woman's facial features, especially her eyes. Women tend to wear the mask on all occasions (except when washing), removing it only for their husbands or, sometimes, their male children (Kanafani 1983).

Omani Dress

Among women's clothing, Oman features the most variety in color and style, with regions having hallmark costumes. The *abaya* and *shayla* are worn in areas near the UAE and in Muscat, but otherwise, Omani fashion little resembles other areas of the Gulf. Women also wear a *hijab*, which is sometimes called a *lihaf*. Embroidery and heavy, engraved silver necklaces, cuffs, and rings are commonly used to adorn the dress and its wearer. In some regions, such as the Sharqiyah, women wear gold jewelry; each finger has a ring with a different name. The embroidery on some dresses and pants is so elaborate that it can take up to two months to complete.

In the Musandam and al-Dhahirah regions, women wear the *kandoura*, which closely resembles the *abaya* but with embroidery around the neck.

In Musandam, an overlay of chiffon, considered to be an *abaya*, covers the *kandoura*. The *burqa* and *shayla* are commonly found in these areas. Otherwise, the most common form of clothing is a brightly colored tunic-dress (*thoub*) that is worn over narrow-legged pants, or *haaf*. In the Muscat, Batinah, and Dhakiliyah regions, women wear very brightly colored ensembles of narrow pants, tunics, and head coverings. The *thoubs* are often in reds, oranges, yellows, and blues and adorned with heavy embroidered bands of cloth or metal thread. Head coverings are also colored and often have tassels gracing the ends; a thin *shayla* might also be worn over the head scarf and across the body. In the Sharqiyah region, women wear a silk *thoub* with embroidered sleeves over narrow pantaloons. Over the *thoub*, the woman wears a *gab'a*, which resembles an *abaya* but is shorter, coming to the waist, and embroidered with front and back panels. Women in the Dhofar region sport a unique dress called the *abu dhail* (colloquially, "one with the tail") because it is shorter in the front than in the back. Made from velvet or cotton, it is often highly embellished. In many of the regions, an *abaya* is not worn when leaving the house; rather, a large rectangle of fabric, often brightly colored, is worn over the hair and wrapped around the body.[1]

Male Dress

Male everyday dress also differs from state to state and between Bedouin and urban dwellers, although most variation is in details such as cuffs, collars, and weight of cloth. The most common form of male dress is the dishdasha, which is sometimes called a *thoub* or *kandoura*. The dishdasha is a one-piece dress that closes at the neck and is slipped over the head. Unlike the *abaya*, the dishdasha is not worn over street clothes as an outer garment, but rather, as a single item of clothing. Under the dishdasha, men wear different types of underclothing but almost always a T-shirt. Usually, the dishdasha comes to a man's ankles, but in some parts of the Gulf, men wear the dishdasha slightly shorter. With the *kandoura*, men wear sandals for everyday use or dark socks and shoes for dress and official occasions. For men, national dress is so synonymous with the dishdasha and sandals that many nightclubs have a "no sandals" or "no local dress" rule because alcohol is served.

Like the *abaya*, dishdashas are individually tailored and purchased from tailoring stores that stock numerous rolls of material in different textures and fabrics. Usually, dishdashas are made from cotton, as silk is *haram* for men, according to Islamic law. White or cream are the most common colors for dishdashas, although tan and shades of light brown are also evident. In Oman, men tend to wear more colorful dress, and thus one sees dishdashas in lavender and other colors. While the *abaya* is a garment that drapes over a woman's body and flows as she moves, dishdashas are pressed so that they fall in a continuous sheet over the man. City dwellers tend to have more tailored *thoubs* with heavy starching, seams, and pockets. Bedouin wear less finished dishdashas that enable them to move more freely because of the absence of plackets, starch, and cuffs.

Although the white dishdasha symbolizes equality among men, variations exist according to country, class, and heritage. While there are general patterns, men frequently more and more choose styles that suit their tastes. The key to deciphering the identity of the wearer lies in an examination of colors, collars, plackets, cuffs, and tassels. For example, shirt collars, plackets with buttons, and fold-over cuffs were commonly associated with Saudi Arabia, but now, one can find such tailored details in other countries, as well. In the UAE and Qatar, men tend to wear round collars with loose sleeves without cuffs, but that is also changing. Men might also signify their tribal background by sporting from their collar a long tassel that trails down the front of the *thoub*. In Oman, men also wear tassels, but they are on the side and used for perfuming.

During the winter months, men choose dark-colored *thoubs* in blue, black, gray, and brown. While the styling remains generally the same, winter dress differs from summer clothing on a number of levels. Unlike white dishdashas that are made from lightweight cotton, winter *thoubs* come in wool fabrics, providing warmth during cool winter days and nights. Many people perceive the usage of fabric dyes as un-Islamic, and thus wool *thoubs* tend toward brown or indigo colors. In the modern age of air-conditioning and climate-controlled architecture, the change from white to colored and woolen fabrics signals a shift in season. Men also trade in their sandals for closed-toe shoes and socks.

For formal and ceremonial events, men layer different types of outer garments over the *thoubs*. Blazers are normally worn over the dishdasha for business events or when the temperature dips. At formal events and special occasions, a man might wear a lightly spun robe of black or gold thread called a *bisht* or *mishlah*. Loosely worn over the *thoub*, the *bisht* is transparent and decorated with golden embroidery. During a ceremony, it is easy to spot rulers and important men because they wear the *bisht*, while other male spectators and lesser members of the entourage sport only the *thoub*.

For Bedouin men, traditional dress is not complete without the *khanjar*, a six- to eight-inch sheathed knife with a horn handle that is worn on a belt around the waist. In earlier periods, the *khanjar* was a working tool used for defensive purposes. Today, men wear the *khanjar* for ornamental and status purposes, although most knifes still retain a very sharp blade. The *khanjar*'s wooden scabbard features detailed silver work down the shaft, which ends in a *J* curve so that the blade of the knife will not perforate the sheath and cause injury to the wearer. Modern fabrication also includes other forms of metalwork, most often in gold.

Male Head Attire

Like women, men in the Gulf cover their heads. Most men outside of Oman wear a *ghutra*, which is a square piece of cotton that is folded into a triangular shape and worn over the *tagiyah*, a small, tightly fitting skullcap that helps fix the *ghutra* in place. While the *tagiyah* can be worn alone, men do not commonly do so in the Gulf. Under the *ghutra*, the *tagiyah* is always white, although it comes in other colors; often, it is perforated with a look that resembles crochet work. *Ghutras* come in white and mixed-color combinations of black, dark green, and red, which have a somewhat checkered appearance. However, there are some customary practices in selecting *ghutras*. The *ghutra* worn in Qatar and the UAE is usually white or checkered red and white, which is also called a *shmagh*, while Kuwaiti and Bahraini men prefer solid white *ghutras*. The *ghutra* provides protection from the blistering sun, and during sandstorms, it can be wound around the face to protect it from blowing sand and debris.

Ghutras are kept in place by placing an *iqal*, or doubled black cord made from tightly woven goat hair or sheep wool, on top of the head. The *iqal* is meant to sit loosely around the crown of the head and not wind tightly around like a headband. Some men, especially young men and Bedouin, choose not to secure the *ghutra* with an *iqal*, but instead wind the ends around, tucking them into the main body of the headdress. Some young men forego the *ghutra* completely, instead donning baseball caps.

Omani men do not wear the *ghutra*, *iqal*, or *taqiyah*, but turbans, or *mussar*, and brightly colored, embroidered caps, or *kummah*. Unlike the other Gulf states, where men sport similarly colored head coverings, Omani men's colored turbans and caps reflect their personal tastes and regions. The *kummah* is larger than the *tagiyah* and with more tailored and rigid sides so that the cap sits on top of the head. Perhaps the most identifiable symbol of Omani male head covering is the turban, which is usually purchased already wound together and then placed on the head like a hat. The finest turbans are made from Kashmiri woven fabrics, which reflect historical trade routes with India. Today, turbans continue to be made from Kashmiri wool, but these are exceedingly expensive, and thus other woolens are substituted. Sultan Qaboos, the ruler of Oman, has a special pattern of turban that is reserved only for members of the royal family.

In a number of Arab Gulf states, companies require employees to wear either company-provided or company-regulated uniforms. For many employees, uniforms are part of the employment package, and employees cannot refuse the clothing. The occupation and status of an individual is readily noticeable by his or her uniform. Construction, cleaning, and maintenance companies brand their uniforms by style, color, and logo. For example, when driving by construction sites at the end of the day, laborers sporting different-colored work clothing can be seen waiting for company busses to return them to their accommodations. Each group of laborers wears the unique clothing of their company, which also serves to indicate the jobs the individuals hold. Security guards wear tailored uniforms with details reminiscent of the military such as epaulets, caps, and wide waistbands. Maids, whether Muslim or not, usually wear loose clothes and *hijabs*. Professionals don Western business attire, although south Asian clothing for women is also deemed appropriate for the business environment.

BODILY ADORNMENT

Kohl, Henna, and Tattoos

Although women use commercial makeup, it was customary for a woman in previous years to adorn only the visible areas of her body, namely, the eyes, hands, and feet. Kohl is a type of eye paint that is also considered to have health implications for everything from poor eyesight to swelling. Kohl is usually applied with a stylus to the outside edges of the eyes or rubbed into the eyebrows. Because it enhances the eyes and is considered a cosmetic, it is avoided during mourning periods. Among the Bedouin, both men and women use kohl, keeping it in small metal containers and decorated bags.

Henna is a popular form of bodily decoration and hair treatment used by women. Made by mixing the dried leaves of the henna plant with water, henna stains the skin a brownish orange color and leaves a reddish sheen on hair. Like kohl, it is considered to possess both aesthetic and health aspects. Sometimes so-called Sudanese henna, or black henna, is used, but since this pigment does not derive from the henna plant, it is considered to be very unhealthy. Henna is used as a hair mask to impart shine and condition the hair. On cuticles, fingernails, palms, and soles of the feet, it is thought to both beautify and nourish dry skin. Henna enables the user to decorate her body with intricate designs without the permanence of tattoos. While primarily considered a woman's treatment, men also used to use henna. When pearl diving, men would apply henna to their hands and the soles of their feet to condition the skin and prevent chapping (Kanafani 1983). Women use henna both for everyday and festive occasions; during weddings and Id feasts, women seek out especially elaborate designs.

As a body art, henna tattoos produce a reddish orange stain on the skin that lasts between six and twelve days. Often, oil is used to anoint the skin after a henna application to further condition the skin and deepen the color of the stain. The dried leaves are ground into a paste and mixed with lemon juice or strong tea to produce a spreadable substance that is squeezed out of a tube or a syringe to form fine, intricate patterns. For very fine patterns, a matchstick is dipped into the paste and used as a paintbrush. Henna is most commonly applied to the hands, palms of the hands, fingernails, and soles and tops of the feet in floral and abstract patterns that extend up the limbs. Some women also apply henna as a tattoo in other areas, usually the back, which affords a large canvas for intricate designs. Arab designs are usually large floral patterns, although *mehndi* designs, which originate from south Asia, are also popular. With the *mehndi* pattern, fine lines create geometric and abstract designs of great detail. Once the patterns have been drawn on the body, the paste must dry for at least thirty minutes, but most women prefer to leave it on for many hours. The longer the henna stays on the skin in paste form, the deeper the

A Muslim woman from the Emirates has her hands decorated with henna. Henna is used in the Islamic world by woman to beautify themselves. © Andrew Holbrooke/ Corbis.

staining. After the paste dries, it is scraped off the skin, leaving a pattern that will darken over days to a reddish brown color.

In some parts of the Gulf, tattoos are also used to enhance a woman's beauty. Geometric simple tattoos in bluish black colors are sometimes seen on the chins and faces of women, especially those in the Omani interior. Islam prohibits tattooing and thus the practice most likely reflects regional and traditional variations of bodily adornment. Today, it is very uncommon for women to have tattoos. It is unclear from the literature how widespread the practice of facial tattoos is or in which areas it continues today.

Modern Accessories

As with *abayas* and *thoubs*, with which fine details confer status and distinction to the wearer, accessories can make or break an individual's style, especially among young, fashion-conscious locals who pay close attention to the latest styles, brand names, and trends. Having the first or only edition of a hot list item distinguishes the owner, especially in Qatar and the UAE. For example, young women frequent bead shops and designer outlets, purchasing baubles to hang off of their mobile phones or Swarovski crystals to apply to phone casings in coordinated and decorative patterns. Men might opt for the latest Mont Blanc pen or an expensive watch. Regardless of what the accessory might be, its prestige value stems from its uniqueness and newness as well as its reference to a particular desired designer.

Young women spend a great deal of money purchasing or customizing purses and computer bags with eye-catching details such as gold chains, appliqués of crystals or fabric, and bold colors. Many women joke that even if a woman is wearing a *niqab*, they can recognize her by the bag she carries, as each bag makes a unique identity statement. Even if a woman does not purchase a high-end designer purse, her accessory can be seen as special if it is unique or if she somehow changes its appearance to suit her personality. Older city women opt less for fanciful and more for designer, high-end bags, but still, the rule of searching for the most unique item applies. The region's many shopping malls cater to this logic of accessory status with specialty stores selling pricey purses, mobile phones, and jewelry. In many cities, one can also buy imitation designer bags, although it is claimed that on close inspection, a discerning individual can separate the authentic from the imitation.

Most locals, men and women, carry at least one mobile phone. Three things set apart mobile phones: the uniqueness of the phone number, the brand, and the style of the phone. Numbers are reputed to have unique values, and people choose their phone numbers according to patterns of numbers, and pay accordingly. For example, phone numbers such as 1122334 or 2224444 would be seen as prestige numbers with high price tags, while numbers such as

5537690 would be seen as randomly generated numbers by phone companies and thus relatively valueless. A so-called good phone number can cost in the thousands of dollars, and thus people keep their numbers for life, trade with each other, and circulate the news of when a hot number will soon be on the market.

The make and model of a phone are also important, with internationally recognized mobile phone manufacturers being the most desirable. People use their mobile phones as more than telephones and thus seek additional features such as cameras, MP3 players, SMS and MMS (multimedia messaging) capabilities, Bluetooth, and scheduling features. In addition to seeking feature-packed phones, locals want the latest model, even if the price tag for such newness is steep. Once a new model emerges, owners visit mobile shops, where they trade in or sell their old phones to the used-phone market.

For men and, to a lesser extent, women, pens are also a status accessory. For men, gold is considered *haram,* and thus entire ranges of fine pens are produced in platinum and silver. Likewise, gemstones are not considered appropriate for men. However, some men do not consider carrying a pen to be wearing an item, and thus there is flexibility and variety in the pens men carry. Status items, such as Mont Blanc, are common with people noting new styles that are promoted for the Islamic market.

NOTE

1. See http://www.omanet.com/ or http://omanpocketguide.com/ for further discussion.

6

Gender, Marriage, and Family

INTRODUCTION

THE BASE OF society in the Gulf states is the family, which, in this case, translates to the larger extended family or tribe. Tribes are pyramidal in structure, with older generations receiving more respect and holding authority. They emphasize both the uniqueness and status of individuals as well as the supportive base of familial connections. Without family, individuals literally would be cut off from daily social life and would also find themselves without the ties needed for success in marriage and business. Daily life in the Gulf states revolves around people's networks, with a large amount of time spent socializing with and visiting family and friends. Reciprocal relationships, in which gender, marital status, family name, and age dictate behavior and expectations, reinforce the continuity and cohesiveness of local communities. People value individual and group relationships, social roles, a code of public behavior, and the importance of family in daily exchanges.

On one hand, society's outward face reflects processes of modernization, yet on the other hand, society is still deeply rooted in traditions, especially those pertaining to family, gender, and marriage. There are deep conflicts between modern values, which emphasize individualism, and traditional values, which accentuate religion and custom as controls for social behavior. Unsurprisingly, there are great generational differences in attitudes and behaviors, as younger generations have grown up with both the benefits and perils of modernization. In the past, men toiled as fishers, pearl divers, or traders—all occupations that took men away from the home for long periods of time. Likewise, a woman was expected to devote her life to the household, raising children, preparing food, and tending to daily matters, often all within the boundaries of her home and neighborhood. Today, with increases in urbanization and settlement, the development of new neighborhoods across stretches of cities, expanded educational opportunities, greater reliance on domestic labor, and changing gender roles, daily life is radically different, although family and tradition remain highly valued. One finds both men and women pursuing education, employed in a wide variety of jobs, utilizing new technologies, and engaging in new social patterns. These changes are most marked among youth, who are often bilingual or more proficient in English, pursue advanced degrees in both local and international universities, worry about costs and prospects of marriage and housing, and have expectations of living a life that is modern, yet culturally appropriate.

FAMILY

Family is the fundamental building block of Gulf societies. When someone speaks about his or her family, it could mean the immediate nuclear family, but more commonly, it refers to the much larger network in which the person belongs: the tribe. Tribes, which comprise clans, signify patrilineage, or the male line of descent. Nearly all nationals belong to a tribe, which can include thousands of people. While people do not necessarily know all members of their family, one can tell to which clan or tribal group someone belongs by his or her family name. Tribes have a pyramidal shape, with the top position occupied by the tribe, and then branching off this are the clans. Within each clan group are found different families. Likewise, genealogy trees are also triangular in shape, with elder generations taking the top positions and branching into the younger generations as one moves down the chart. Within the tribe, the term *cousin* refers to those who occupy the same branch level of the kinship tree. *Cousin* can be used to identify someone who is a first cousin or someone else of the family with a much more distant relationship. These family trees tell one literally to whom one belongs—both in the immediate bloodline and within the larger family picture. Tribes always reference the male descent line; women maintain the family name on marriage but give birth to children who belong to their husbands' families.

Historically, each tribe had a ruling sheikh as well as its own territory, across which the tribe moved during winter and spring and in which they settled in summer (with water coming from wells, springs, or oases). The sheikh was a respected individual chosen from the ruling family because of personal qualities for leadership. The sheikh was always male (*sheikha* is the corresponding female term), and on his death, a successor was chosen who also exemplified leadership. Even today, succession is through the bloodline, with fathers cultivating leadership within their sons; often the eldest son will assume the leadership role, but not always, as a history of sons overthrowing their fathers (e.g., Oman and Qatar) and younger brothers assuming leadership (e.g., the United Arab Emirates, UAE) is documented across the Gulf. Depending on the benevolence of the sheikh, other tribes were permitted to pass through a tribe's territory for trade or to utilize its water sources.

Today, the nation-state seeks to inculcate a sense of national identity among locals to supplant, or at least augment, tribal identity and membership as the means for social organization and allegiance. While the state possesses most of the political authority that previously belonged to the tribe (ruling families and sheikhs continue today), tribes continue to play a large role in both an individual's life and the overall social fabric. A person's tribal affiliation tells the person whether he or she is from a Bedouin tribe, an Arab tribe from Iran, or a trader family. Although daily life revolves less around one's kinsmen than years past, the tribe still influences an individual's status, possibilities for marriage partners, business opportunities, land rights, and heritage. For example, in Bahrain, modernization has eroded aspects of the tribal system, with class and other factors emerging as newly defined markers of identity, yet tribalism is still invoked to confirm heritage. Families enjoy varying amounts of *wasta*, which roughly translates into "connections of influence." *Wasta* is an important form of power within the Gulf: it both opens and closes doors, and thus one's family background remains of paramount importance.

Generally, residence follows patrilocal patterns, where couples live with the man's family. In much of the Gulf, multiple generations compose a household. For example, most Kuwaitis live in extended households for economic and familial reasons, as do Omanis, where the eldest male has authority in the household. Qataris, though, live in everything from nuclear to extended households. When given the opportunity, they prefer to live near family, as do Emiratis, who nearly all live in nuclear households.

Families cherish children and desire many of them. In past years, having families with more than five children, and especially a large number of sons, accorded prestige and honor. This is not to say that daughters are unwanted, especially nowadays, but rather, male children are often desired as they stay within the family and carry greater social value. It is not unheard of to hear of women with more than ten children, but today, it is more usual to have between three and five children. However, when a man has more than one wife, the number of children in the household can be quite large and span great age differences. In the case of households with more than one wife, the children from the same mother tend to be closer to each other than to their half siblings. Adoption tends not to be practiced, although families sometimes foster children, noting that while it is important to care for children without parents, it is equally important for a child to know from which background he or she originates, especially in a tribal society.

Often, families employ a range of domestic servants to assist with child raising and household chores; children may have maids assigned to them, who accompany them to school and on other outings outside the house, especially in the case of daughters. On divorce, it is customary for children to remain with the mother until a specified age and, after that age, to live with the father. While this is the preferred arrangement, as children belong to the man's family, it is not unheard of for the children to remain with the mother or, in some cases, be completely raised by the father and his family. This practice differs among tribal groups and states. For example, in Oman, a child, when reaching two years old, is considered a miniature adult and socialized into community life by taking on adult activities in areas such as hospitality. In the UAE, a child changes status around five years old, after which childlike behavior is no longer tolerated.

From an early age, boys and girls are socialized differently, often in segregated environments. Previously, parents celebrated the birth of a son, but not necessarily the birth of a daughter, unless the parents had planned an event regardless of the sex of the child, although this occurs less often now. Growing up, sons often have more leisure time for play, while daughters shoulder adult responsibilities such as helping with household chores or caring for younger siblings. This pattern continues into adulthood, when sons have greater freedom to socialize with friends, while daughters are often expected to remain around the house, unless an activity seen as valuable is happening outside of the house such as education or work.

Names are very important in Gulf society. Written into each person's name is his or her lineage history, starting with the father and ending with the family or tribal name. For example, a woman might be named Hind Mohammed Ibrahim Suleiman al-Jasim; Mohammed is her father, Ibrahim denotes her grandfather, Suleiman is her great grandfather, and al-Jasim signifies her family. Given names are sex-specific (it is rare to find a given name that both men and women share), while only male names are used to denote the family line (as Gulf societies are patrilineal), and can include five or more generations. Some families have thousands of members—only from knowing a full name can one know exactly which individual is in question. Many families cycle through names and keep a family tree that displays the given names within the family. For foreigners, this can be quite confusing. On one hand, given names are commonly used, often with the appropriate title attached, in both formal and informal situations. For example, one might see Dr. Mouna in a medical office or meet Mr. Suleiman for a business appointment. It is also customary for the parents to adopt the child's name in combination with umm (mother) or abu (father). Thus a couple that names their first child Basem will afterward be known as Umm Basem and Abu Basem.

GENDER

Gender roles are deeply differentiated within the Gulf states; men and women are conceptualized as fundamentally distinct, but with potentially equal capacities. In general, even with the influence of modernization, there are trends toward conservatism with regard to gender experimentation and sexuality. Homosexuality, transsexualism, transvestitism, and premarital sexual relations are illegal and not tolerated. Likewise, men and women are expected to behave within their associated gender codes. Gender ideologies not only dictate specific roles for men and women to adopt, but also shape cultural and religious beliefs that structure men's and women's rights, access to resources, and mobility in society.

Popular images of the Arabian Gulf abound with stereotyped representations of gender: veiled women lounging in harem settings or peeking through fences and headdress-swathed men riding horses or camels across endless sand dunes. The contrast between these images, which fill romantic paintings and movies, and the sex-gender system of the Gulf is striking. Today, there are increasingly flexible ideas about gender in response to external pressures from modernization and internal cultural changes that seek greater participation of women in public. Gender is in flux and, with each generation, is changing. Consequently, in one family, you might find a woman working as a teacher and balancing the demands of motherhood, while in another household, the women might not work. Today, men and women meet in a wide variety of social and professional settings, and thus new ideas of gender are emerging that take into account societal change, but also may reflect entrenched gendered roles and expectations.

In general, Arab society recognizes two genders that correspond to the biological sex of men and women. Men possess greater authority in nearly all aspects of society. They serve as legal guardians of women, who are perceived as weaker and in need of protection. As a daughter, a woman is a father's responsibility; as a wife, she falls under her husband's authority; and as an unmarried older woman, she will fall under a brother's custodianship. In public, women are expected to be accompanied by an appropriate guardian. This holds true even for professional women who attend public events. Guardianship is not simply a cultural matter, but also a legal one, as evident in women needing male permission for travel or sponsorship of a business endeavor. The rationale behind guardianship lies in cultural ideas that women are weak and thus a woman's virtue must be protected from the advances, inappropriate behaviors, and gaze of men, especially those who might possibly be construed as marriage partners.

Women work but are seen first as mothers and wives who look after children, prepare food, and manage daily household activities. For many women, marriage and motherhood are all-consuming activities. Thus they choose not to work or are prevented from doing so by men in their families, who often perceive women's work outside the home as unnecessary and potentially damaging. A woman must get married to function as a fully socially accepted individual in society (although there are some exceptions). A woman's married life revolves around the family, preparing meals, and tending to children. Men are expected to provide for the family and make major household decisions as well as those pertaining to children. Fathers often spend time with their children, interacting with warmth and affection and providing authoritative guidance on all matters from education to marriage.

Although popular ideas portray women in need of guidance and men as providers, the essentialism that constructs the social categories of "man" and "woman" also frames them as complementary. The late Sheikh Zayed, former president of the UAE, once noted that the woman is the right arm of the man. Consequently, there are very few feminist or other movements that propose the idea that men and women should have absolute equality. In general, the rigidity of gender categories is accepted. While there are other categories, such as eunuchs, who were traditionally employed to sing for men at weddings, little gender bending occurs outside of one's sex. Not only is it discouraged for men to act like women and for women to act like men, but also, it is illegal in many contexts. Aberrations of gender are taken quite seriously—even donning the other sex's traditional dress is frowned on (although women do wear jeans). While the male thoub and the female abaya might look similar to a Western eye—both are dresslike gowns that cover the body modestly—a man would never wear women's clothing or vice versa. Subtle changes in gendered behavior are emerging. For example, ten years ago in Qatar, men used to walk a few steps in front of their wives. Now it is not uncommon to see couples in shopping malls strolling side by side and even holding hands. Strong notions of what constitutes a man or woman as an honorable human dictate expectations of gender roles, spaces, and behaviors, but these ideas are also in flux.

Throughout the Gulf, sex segregation is practiced in everything from education to the arrangement of space inside the house, providing a window into how gender is both conceptualized and practiced as a system of social organization. Throughout the Middle East, the public and private are considered separate and gendered spaces. As the public sphere is the space of politics, commerce, and authority, it is often associated with men. Similarly, the private is perceived of as a controlled space of domesticity and is thus linked to women. The organization of physical space also translates into the ways social space is organized: people tend to socialize within same-sex groups.

While men have authority in both spaces, women often possess a great deal of power within the home. Men entertain their guests in male-only *majlises*, which are places for socializing and conducting business. These *majlises* often have their own entrance or a door at the front of the house to prevent males from entering the domestic space of the house. Women have their own salons or areas for receiving their guests. By enclosing female space, unwanted male attention can be prevented and female honor preserved. At home, women do not wear the *abaya* or *shayla* (although sometimes they do for entertaining), instead choosing other forms of dress and hair covering. Likewise, when men are not being entertained in the men's *majlis*, women move freely throughout the house and its compound, often in rooms or courtyards that are separated from public areas. Outside the home, women often adopt local dress, which involves covering all or part of the face. Older women, especially Bedouin, don the *burqa*, or facial mask, as a way to maintain an area of space around them and avert male eyes from their faces.

While this is a general overview of space and its gendered associations, in practice, the boundedness of these spaces comes into question as increasingly, they are becoming more fluid spaces in much of the Gulf, especially Bahrain, Kuwait, Qatar, and the UAE. Women are increasingly entering politics and the workplace in all Gulf countries, arenas that were previously within the domain of men. In states such as Bahrain, where women have not been as successful politically or in securing civil rights, advancements in health, education, and employment are evident (Seikaly 1994). Historically, women have also entertained varying degrees of power. In Oman, for example, women have always had personal status, and throughout Bedouin communities, women have been admired for their fortitude and cleverness. Many welcome modern changes that place women centrally in the public eye, viewing change not as a transgression of women venturing into male space, but rather as a way to meet rising daily costs and create a developed society in which people have flexibility in social roles. In Qatar, Sheikha Moaza, the wife of Emir Thani, is greatly respected for her pursuit of education and the development of institutions of higher learning. However, this is not to suggest that women who break boundaries do not come under fierce public scrutiny or cultural obstacles in achieving their goals. For example, Sheikha Lubna, the first female minister in the UAE federal cabinet, is both admired for her business savvy and scrutinized for being a single woman. Likewise, the Jordanian wife of

Sheikh Mohammed of Dubai, Princess Haya, is regularly criticized for neither wearing appropriate dress nor behaving modestly around her husband,
despite her achievements in sport and humanitarian activities. Female ministers and politicians across the Gulf have noted that even with opening doors,
the place of politics is still exceptionally male. In Kuwait, women received the
right to vote, but recent years have shown that women's acceptance in politics is still troublesome for society. Many meetings occur in a *majlis* context,
which is still limited to men. Like so-called golf course meetings, these are
not formal affairs, but rather informal locations, where power is wielded and
decisions are made.

Despite more women entering the public sphere and men participating
in daily household activities, sex segregation is still commonly practiced and
preferred. Government educational institutions are all single sex, even at the
university level, although male and female campuses might be part of the same
institution. Likewise, weddings are held with separate male and female parties,
rather than one large, joint party for the bride and groom. Summer camps and
youth organizations are also single sex, as are many recreational areas, such as
malls and beaches, which often have women-only or family days that afford
women leisure time outside the presence of men. During Ramadan, many
young men move from their homes to the desert, spending their evenings
with friends and male family members. These encampments are exclusively
male spaces. There are some cross-sex friendships, but they are unusual and
often limited to phone or e-mail communication, in part to preserve the virtue
of women and in recognition of the authority of men. While men and women
recognize that segregation and gender distinctness is a key attribute of Arabian
culture, others attribute this to religious values of modesty.

To many Western observers and critics from within the Arab world, the
hareem system—the extension of the women's quarters in a household into
a system where women are either relegated in public space or segregated—
is an oppressive system. As with other aspects of gendered stereotypes, the
situation on the ground is much more complicated. For example, the perimeter walls that surround many educational institutions allow women to unveil
and behave according to their own preferences—outside the gaze of family
members—and thus afford them measures of independence and possibilities for individual freedom. Likewise, it has been suggested that fully veiled
women enjoy anonymity and thus freedom of movement, as their identity is
obscured. In the Gulf, strategies to avert (primarily) the male gaze take many
forms, from the burqa that older women favor to the almost black tinting
on automobiles, which completely prevents people from looking inside and,
according to local common sense, wards off undesired attention and potential harassment, and marks the individual as honorable. While these strategies

regulate women's bodies, spaces, and behaviors, it is important to note that they are often tactics employed by women themselves to move freely outside their homes. Reputation is of critical importance to all people, men and women, and thus abiding by social custom is one way to achieve personal goals, yet show one's cultural awareness and fluency.

It is worth noting that today's women lead radically different lives than those of previous generations, due in part to modern conveniences such as air-conditioning and motorized vehicles, changes in employment structures, availability and affordability of household servants, and access to education. In many ways, heightened attitudes toward segregation reflect a changing society in which gender roles and opportunities are more fluid and flexible. Before the advent of oil and the development of commerce and service industries, the economy of the Gulf states revolved around pearl diving and trading, while Bedouin moved between encampments. Pearl divers and fishermen often left home for large parts of the year, leaving women to tend to household matters in addition to raising children. Among the Bedouin, many hard tasks, such as weaving and pitching the heavy goat hair tents, were seen as women's work. Clearly the conception that women were not active members of the household with many responsibilities in addition to child rearing is simply not true and more a product of Western ideas of "exotic" Arabia.

Gendered Practices

While children belong to the father's lineage and fathers eagerly await the birth of a child, birthing practices are clearly the domain of women. Today, women give birth in hospitals as well as using midwives. There is little information about cultural practices for mother and child after the birthing process. Emirati popular lore says that boys emerge face up and girls face down. Once born, Emirati babies are wrapped in linen and fed a mixture of clarified butter and date syrup to clean their intestines after birth. After three days, the mother begins breast-feeding and continues for two years. For the first forty days after birth, the infant remains with the mother and after that time is reincorporated into the family. During this period, husband and wife also refrain from sexual intercourse. Salt therapy is applied to both mother and child. For the newborn infant, a rub of salt and other substances is applied after birth. For the mother, salt serves as a cleansing mechanism that purifies the woman, removing old blood and dirt. It is believed that without salt suppositories, an infection will develop and harm the mother's health. For forty days, the woman's body is considered impure, and thus she abstains from activities such as wearing perfume (Kanafani 1983, 262–266). During menstruation, women are also considered impure, as the distinction is made between flowing and stagnant blood.

Both men and women take pride in the aesthetics of the body. One manner of adorning the body is through the use of perfume, which has a long history in Arabia. In just about every mall, Arabian perfume outlets cater to individual tastes, selling everything from incense to aromatic oils in both pure and blended forms. Many of these oils are extremely expensive, as much as the finest perfumes found worldwide. The scent of Arabian perfume is very strong, originating from various woods as well as natural sources. It is quite common to layer scents, beginning with oils and then enhancing the aromas with the smoke from incense.

It is believed that perfume should be applied to clean skin not only to enhance aroma, but also to ensure good health. Oils can be used on just about every part of the body, but especially in the hair, near the ears, on the neck, under the arms, and on the nose. Incense, prized for its aroma, is used to perfume clothing and homes and especially so on festive and ritual occasions. When women host guests, they pass around a *mabkhara*, or incense burner, filled with *bukhoor*, or wood-chip bricks scented with oils, which their guests use to fumigate and scent their clothes, first holding it under their hems, moving it toward their sleeves, and then drawing wafts of smoke to their hair and necklines. At home, incense burners are placed in closets and *majlises*, allowing the scents to drift and permeate fabric. Exceptions to perfuming are for health or religious reasons: the sickly avoid scents, a menstruating woman or new mother refrains from oils and incense, and people abstain from them during Ramadan days.

Oils are often favored and derive from a variety of sources. In the UAE, the most prized oil is aloe wood oil, which is imported from India; aloe wood oil is also the most expensive (upward of $150/ounce), with price dependent on quality. One of the oldest scents is that of frankincense, which is a resin excreted from the *Boswellia serrata* tree. Frankincense is primarily used as protection against the evil eye, although it can also be chewed to freshen the breath and added as a scent to drinking water, which it also purifies due to its germicidal properties. Oman is known for its trade in frankincense, although it can be purchased throughout the Gulf. Many women have collections of perfumes that they keep in perfume boxes, displaying their scents for others to admire and for the owner to mix on her body. Men tend to favor aloe wood oil as the traditional scent of choice.

Women also adorn their bodies with jewelry. While gold is associated with coastal and urban areas, Bedouin often favor silver jewelry, although today, gold is in fashion for all, as are precious stones. Only married women are allowed to wear certain types of jewelry and perfume, and thus the wedding party is the place par excellence to display one's riches and also for the bride to adorn herself in items that signal her new status. Jewelry covers the bride from head to toe, both decorating her body and indicating relative wealth and status. Perhaps the best-known item of wedding jewelry is the *al-tasa*, which is a circular piece of gold with chains and stones hanging from the side. It circles the bride's head and appears similar to a golden crown. She might also wear different gold necklaces, such as the *al-murta'isha*, which is a necklace of gold with inlaid jewels, and bracelets, earrings with stones, anklets, and rings on her fingers and toes. Gold jewelry was often imported from India, serving as both an important item in local rituals and in economic transactions. Men do not wear jewelry or items that could be construed as such, as Islam prohibits it. However, men do wear watches and cuff links, which are considered utilitarian items with aesthetic value.

Gendered Institutions

Until recent decades, women's education was virtually unknown. Women were expected to be illiterate and uneducated, as education was often limited to males and women's roles in society were limited to housewives and mothers. However, with modernization, governments began not only to offer, but also to mandate women's education, at first through primary school levels and, today, through secondary school. However, in some areas, notably rural areas of Oman, women do not finish secondary school because of marriage. Still, all countries in the Gulf have numerous schools and the goal of high literacy rates for men and women. In Qatar, public schooling began in the 1950s, and institutions of higher education opened in the 1970s. The first university in Oman opened in the 1980s. Government schools are all sex segregated and, in some cases, have gender-tailored curricula—Qatar had separate curricula for boys and girls until the 1970s. Opportunities exist for older women as many women's associations promote literacy education for women of all ages. Today, women attend college, acquire university diplomas, and pursue graduate degrees in both private and government institutions of higher education. Without the support of ruling families, many of whom embrace the education of locals as part and parcel of the development of the nation, families would not encourage women to pursue higher education. In most states, women surpass the educational level of men and have higher graduation rates from local universities. This is due in part to the pressure men feel to begin a career or serve in the military. It also arises from more men than women attending universities in foreign countries.

In addition to the development of local universities and colleges, many foreign universities are setting up campuses across the Gulf. For example, in Kuwait, one finds the American University of Kuwait; in UAE, New York University is starting a campus; and in Qatar, Education City offers majors from top American universities such as Carnegie Mellon and Georgetown.

There are a number of reasons why governments would want to work with foreign institutions in the development of more higher-education programs, even though these offerings directly compete with local institutions of higher education. On one hand, privilege and status are associated with foreign degrees; by bringing foreign institutions to the Gulf, locals can acquire these degrees but stay at home, working to develop their countries. On the other hand, many Gulf states stress that the region is emerging as a knowledge society hub, and thus education takes on primary importance in the battle to combat brain drain in the Arab world. Private, foreign universities cater to both local and expatriate populations.

It is unclear at this stage what the effect of women's education will be on gender roles and social custom. Education affords women the possibility of getting out of the house, as the life of an unmarried woman is often limited to household activities or perhaps shopping excursions with family and friends. Some suggest that a woman's education makes her more marriageable, while others have raised questions as to whether men will want to marry women who have attained higher educational levels than many men. Nearly all colleges and universities in the Gulf emphasize that education is important not only for women's development, but also in the expansion of a local workforce, even if in some countries, such as Bahrain, training programs for women reflect conservative cultural biases. Most higher-education programs are closely tied to market forces, with professional degrees in areas such as teaching, business, media, and education.

Part of the push to educate the local population is due to the presence of large numbers of expatriate workers in all the Gulf states. The question of the effects of expatriate labor on the national labor force is regularly addressed in the press as well as in government policies. From Oman, where there is a small expatriate population, to the UAE, where there is a larger percentage of expatriates, governments are forming nationalization programs that either delineate a specific quota of employees that must be nationals or give priority to national hires over equally qualified expatriates. Even with these policies, countries struggle with under- and unemployment, especially in the private sector. Reasons for local employment problems range from a lack of training and educational programs to cultural differences in work ethics. Most expatriate professionals work on what are termed "expatriate packages" that include housing or an allowance, travel tickets, private education for children, and other benefits. Similarly, there are wage and housing structures for national employees.

Locals work in all sectors, although certain positions are favored, especially those in education, business, and government institutions. Men often work in government institutions and family-owned businesses, although increasingly, they are also working in the private sector. Women tend to be less represented in the private sector, in part because of the longer work hours and the presence of foreign men, but they are quickly catching up to the percentage of men employed in government institutions. Teaching and public sector employment are especially favored professions as they allow shorter hours so women can be at home with the children. Both men and women especially like entrepreneurial activities. It is not unusual for an individual to have a number of entrepreneurships, even at a young age. Other industries, such as medicine, are starting to have Arab Gulf employees, but as there are few medical schools within the Gulf, this area of employment lags behind the others. Finally, as more countries in the Gulf are pursuing elections and expanding ministries, the number of women entering politics is increasing, although their numbers remain quite small in comparison with men. Many women continue working after marriage, although it is anticipated that they will begin to bear children as soon as possible. Despite the reliance on domestic labor and changing attitudes toward women and work, many social, political, and cultural obstacles remain for women's employment. For example, in the UAE, women lag behind men in work, opting instead for motherhood and marriage.

There are few nongovernmental organizations in the Gulf states, in part because the political structures of governance as well as the reliance on family networks and *wasta* do not foster civil society. Voluntary associations, however, flourish and, for the most part, are akin to social clubs organized around leisure, handicrafts, or like activities. For example, men might belong to a male association dedicated to heritage or cultural practices such as dancing or falconry. Women might belong to associations that concentrate on philanthropy or socializing. There are organizations that seek to develop women's capacities. For example, the Women's Association, under the patronage of Sheikha Fatima in the UAE, sponsors literacy among women. Likewise, one can find organizations that offer language and vocational training for older women, as they are often ineligible for university enrollment because of age restrictions. In Kuwait, a few organizations concentrate on the development of women's political rights; the UAE has a small number of informal women's organizations that seek to change laws perceived as detrimental to women at risk (divorced women, women with foreign spouses, and so forth). In general, though, most organizations concentrate on self-help within the confines of the social status quo, rather than on a transformation of political structure.

MARRIAGE

Marriage is both a family and business agreement, with most people favoring arranged, rather than love, marriages. There is a preference for endogamous marriage, or marriage from one's own tribe, which reinforces reciprocity and retains wealth within the same larger family group. Moreover, by seeking prospective spouses "from the family," those arranging the marriage know more about the individual in question. Everything from family reputation, educational level, financial prospects, religiosity, and personal character are taken into consideration. Often, cousins marry, but as families can be quite large and even cross state boundaries, the cousin may or may not be someone the individual has known previously. While the preference for cousin marriage continues, it is changing with younger generations. For example, in Kuwait, educated individuals, upper and middle class, and young people prefer to marry those with similar educational and professional backgrounds, and thus the parents' role changes from direction to consultation.

While it is legal for a man to marry a foreigner, it is preferred that he take a wife from his national community, or at least from another Arab Gulf state. Family is extremely important, and with membership within it comes social obligations and potential interference. Consequently, some men, for example, in Qatar, prefer to marry women from other Gulf states as it significantly frees them from the pressures of extended family obligations. Consequently, local women find themselves with fewer men eligible for marriage. The UAE is seeking to counter this problem with the establishment of a "marriage fund" that encourages men to marry Emirati women, providing them with a fixed sum payment that can significantly offset costs such as bride-price and the wedding. For women, it is much harder to marry nonlocals as they must receive approval from their fathers for the marriage to go forward. Moreover, such unions come at great cost. While women usually do not lose their national rights, they cannot pass them to their children, as the society is based on a patrilineal system; consequently, children from these unions cannot carry the national passport, attend national schools, or claim membership within the tribal community.

In past years, girls were considered marriageable as young as twelve and were nearly always married by eighteen. Nowadays, the preference is for brides who have completed at least secondary, if not university or college, education. In Qatar, the average age of a first marriage for a woman was twenty-three in 2001. Except in the case of remarriage, women are expected to be virgins. Men tend to be older as it is expected that shortly after marriage, they will be able to provide a home and support a growing family.

According to Islamic law, a man can marry up to four wives if he can treat and provide for them equally in all ways, from affection to financial support. Polygyny, or having more than one wife, was more commonly practiced in past decades than today, with younger generations favoring one wife because of financial constraints, changing views of marriage, and rising divorce rates. Still, it is not uncommon for men of prestige, wealth, and power to have more than one wife, often marrying subsequent wives over many years. In these situations, the first wife is usually a close cousin, with subsequent wives being more distant in the family or even outside the family. In polygynous families, children from the same mother tend to be closer to each other. Although Islamic law stipulates that all wives are equal, many women prefer to be the first or only wife.

Dating is virtually nonexistent for Arab Gulf nationals. Instead, a variety of resources are employed in the search for a spouse. Families can get involved and make inquiries, young men can seek out recommendations from friends and family, or young men can ask about women they have seen and found to be attractive. The traditional matchmaker, or *al-khatibah,* is also consulted, especially in situations where an arrangement might be difficult, as in the case of older women past the ideal marrying age, divorcées, and widows and widowers. While relied on heavily in the past, the matchmaker's role is diminishing as opportunities for meeting or learning about potential matches are changing, as social, education, and work networks expand. Although still not as common as in the West, another source for seeking spouses are newspaper ads. Examples from Qatar read, "Qatari young man, 35, religious and God-fearing with a high-ranking job, seeks to marry a young Qatari woman from a respectable family, beautiful, with fair skin and religious" and "Qatari widow, with acceptable appearance, working, religious, from a respected family and an excellent housewife, seeks to marry an educated Qatari man—divorced or widowed—who is God-fearing" (Bahry and Marr 2005, 116).

Often, older female family members of the prospective groom begin looking for a suitable bride from the extended family and circles of friends. At weddings, available females are sometimes displayed in a special area, making known their availability. Women can also signal to their families that they are interested in marriage, but usually, prospective brides do not begin the process. In some families, the girl's female relatives find the prospective spouse, while in other families, it is male relatives or the man's family. Once a prospective bride is found, the father of the groom visits the girl's house; if she agrees, the bride-price, or dowry (*mahr*), is paid, and the dates for the religious and social ceremonies are set. Young people sometimes express the desire for a love match, rather than an arranged match, yet both women and men usually have the option to refuse a prospective partner. Initiation of partnership is not made lightly, as families do not want to be in the position of gaining the reputation that their sons or daughters are in the habit of rejecting potential spouses.

Engagements in the Gulf states are quite different from what one finds in the West. Sometimes there is a small celebration, but the ritual primarily consists of signing the religious marriage contract, or, in the case of some Bedouin tribes, the proclamation of the contract, with the father standing in as the representative of the girl (and the girl listening behind a partition).

While this formality unites the couple legally and in the eyes of the religious community, they are not usually considered married until the union is socially sanctioned by a wedding celebration. When an engagement has been secured, a courtship period might ensue, with the couple socializing in the company of others, shopping for household goods, and, in general, getting to know each other before they are formally married. In some cases, the couple has opportunities to get to know each other through chaperoned meetings and telephone calls before the engagement, allowing either party to call off the marriage without consequence. It is quite unusual today for a couple to marry without having at least limited opportunities for getting to know each other.

Marriage is an expensive prospect. Traditionally, the man's family will pay a bride-price, or *mahr,* to the woman's family before the wedding. One of the problems facing Gulf societies today is the increased cost of bride-prices and the expectation that the groom's family will purchase expensive jewelry for the bride. Sometimes women will keep the *mahr,* but usually, the funds are used to help establish a home for the couple. Moreover, there is the social expectation that weddings will be lavish occasions held in exclusive hotels or clubs. In general, the wedding party consists of a feast for family and friends— men and women have separate wedding parties, sometimes on different days. For women, weddings are times to dress up and sport one's best clothes and jewelry—hairstyles can be elaborate, as can makeup. As the guest list numbers in the hundreds and as men and women hold separate wedding parties, the cost of a wedding can easily range upward from one hundred thousand dollars. Rising bride-prices, expectations, wedding costs, and housing prices across the Gulf result in many couples finding themselves either delaying marriage or living with the man's family until sufficient capital can be amassed either to buy or build a home.

Once the marriage contract is officiated or a wedding period complete, the couple either embarks on a honeymoon, which today can be an elaborate affair, lasting months and involving travel across many countries, or they simply stay alone for a few days. Bedouin would often stay in a specially made tent close to the groom's father's tent or, if the man was remarrying or marrying another wife, a tent within his area; a new bride would not be expected to share the tent with a man's other wives. During the couple's early period together, they are expected to consummate their union. Ideally, this should happen as soon as possible. The newlywed couple is expected to be nervous, as their first night together is the time for the man to display his manliness and for the woman to fend him off and thus exhibit her shyness and virtue. It is not uncommon for stories to circulate about the success of a couple on their wedding night, as people recognize that both bride and groom suffer from tremendous social pressure on the occasion of their wedding.

Previously, divorce was rare, but today, it is a problem, with states experiencing double-digit divorce rates. Couples divorce because of a wide variety of reasons, from the interference of family members to disagreements over money. Many wives complain that men spend too much time outside of the home, and often without explanation (unmarried women also complain that men no longer know how to accept the social responsibilities of marriage). Both men and women can initiate divorce proceedings. Although exceptionally unusual, there have been cases in which men have divorced their wives through SMS text messages, typing "I divorce thee" three times. Regardless of the circumstances surrounding a divorce, women are especially vulnerable afterward, both socially and economically. Divorced women often have trouble remarrying and thus find themselves in a difficult situation, as they return to their natal families.

$$7$$

Social Lives: Custom, Folklore, and the Daily Rhythm

INTRODUCTION

CULTURAL TRADITIONS STEM primarily from the region's Bedouin and trading past—favorite symbols and stories tell of a life dramatically different from the one lived today, with modern conveniences and new forms of community. Throughout the Gulf, the question of cultural continuity is also an inquiry into local identity. Today's fashionistas, for example, have traded in pearls for gold and diamonds as the decorations of choice, yet people continue to value the pearl for its beauty, perceived power, and symbolism. With change happening at every turn, culture stands out as a self-conscious object for preservation and display. What was once a way of life, for instance, falconry, now emerges as an activity distant from its roots and showcased in museums and living culture activities. Similarly, some might still follow folk practices in areas such as medicine, but as modern medicine becomes the standard for health care, this knowledge, too, becomes catalogued as a relic of the past. That said, across the Gulf, people take great pride in their history, beliefs, and ways of life and seek out new ways to keep tradition in the present. Leisure activities combine the best of both worlds, with people engaging in modern sports and participating in traditional cultural activities. Families visit the desert not only to enjoy the respite it provides from urban life, but also to connect to the land that once provided challenges and sustenance to past generations. Camping in the desert reaffirms cultural values of community and family and recalls Bedouin life. Thus the pulse of social life straddles the very questions Gulf locals articulate when they embrace the modern, yet seek ways to preserve cultural traditions that root them to their identity and history.

COMMUNITY

Much of daily life revolves around community, or the familial, national (federal), and local networks and groups that provide a sense of belonging, shared history, and cultural commonality that, in turn, encourage feelings of connection. The idea of blood and social reciprocity form a foundation for ideas of community in the Gulf, especially in constructing in- and out-groups through language, law, and identity. Bedouins and Gulf Arabs are traditionally welcoming to visitors and outsiders. At the same time, outsiders rarely are considered part of community because they cannot access the base on which it is constructed. The large expatriate workforce, foreign domestic help, English usage, and modernization processes exacerbate what many consider to be a loss of traditions and a threat to local community. Regular discussions in the newspapers suggest that a loss of identity follows the increasing complexity of what makes up community. In response to the question of how to revitalize and sustain community identity, governments are setting up heritage centers, living history museums, that foster connections between national identity and Gulf culture.

For older generations, the neighborhood served as the locus for community. In this traditional neighborhood, or *freej*, people had intimate connections not only because living conditions were much closer than the apartments and villas of today, but also because it was the space where social values were reinforced, marriages facilitated, business transactions conducted, and interpersonal relationships nurtured. For many Gulf locals, the traditional community, a hallmark of daily urban life, has come under siege from urbanization, as has the way of life associated with it. Today, many young couples find it difficult to live near family due to housing shortages, high home prices, and the need to relocate because of work. Consequently, one finds locals living in neighborhoods very unlike the *freej*; in the United Arab Emirates (UAE), nationals live among expatriates or build houses in new communities outside the city center, and in Qatar, village populations have been relocated to urban centers that offer more amenities.

To draw attention to the demise of community, Mohammed Harib, an Emirati animator, produced the television cartoon *Freej* in 2006. *Freej*, using the Khaleeji Arabic dialect, tells the story of four older women who live in a traditional neighborhood of Dubai as the city rockets around them. The show illustrates how the women try to come to terms with the rapid changes all around them, translating between old and new ways. Harib's motivation was to address his concerns as well as those of others about the disappearance and change of local custom. Thus the show covers many topics considered uniquely cultural such as night visits of ghosts (djinn), the perils of gossip and conniving women, women's educational programs, the centrality of local shopkeepers, and ritual events. *Freej* debuted as a special program during Ramadan and was received with great fanfare. It has been recently released on DVD (with English subtitles) and has its own line of merchandising.

While Freej uses humor to depict cultural change, many local programs are seeking ways to revitalize culture and address societal development. Parenting awareness programs are cropping up in many adult centers and in media campaigns, encouraging parents to spend time with their children, rather than leave them with a nanny or in front of the television. Arabic poetry contests encourage youth and adults to concentrate on Arabic as a literary form to combat falling Arabic fluency rates, as English becomes the lingua franca. Likewise, heritage villages and museums are increasing in number to highlight historical cultural practices such as pearl diving and falconry, not only for foreigners, but also for local populations. For many, the perceived demographic threat from expatriate populations translates into cultural problems, as people seek ways to articulate a Gulf lifestyle that is both modern and traditional.

Communication technologies also have altered the rhythm and form of interaction among Gulf residents, especially for younger generations. The Gulf market has one of the highest penetrations of mobile phone usage in the Arab world, with people owning multiple numbers for business, pleasure, and even different types of social relationships. People spend significant amounts of time talking and sending text messages on mobile phones. In the case of important breaking news, text messages can broadcast information to a large group of people often before the news agencies carry the same information. Likewise, the mobile phone facilitates convenience in daily services. In some countries, bills can be paid through text message services, and, in most areas, the Internet can be accessed by the latest phones. As mentioned in Chapter 6, even divorce through text message became a possibility. Similarly for young people, Bluetooth technology on mobile phones has become a tool through which individuals send images to one another and affords young people the possibility of flirting privately while in public settings.

Social networking sites enjoy great popularity both among national Gulf Arab and expatriate populations. Facebook, MySpace, Hi5, Orkut, LinkedIn, and others can be found throughout the Gulf. While English is the primary language for these sites, one also finds Arabic-only areas. Within these sites, there are subcommunities that cross national boundaries. People gossip, announce parties, and look for new friends in ways that would be unaccept-able to the traditional community. Often, young Gulf nationals localize these sites by writing spoken Arabic in English letters but not using the rules that govern standard transliteration practices. This form of Arabic, often referred to as Arab English or Arabizi, creates a new code for SMSing and chat that looks unfamiliar to both Arabic and English speakers. Recently, a social net-working site aimed at Muslims, Muxlim.com, was launched in Europe, with the Gulf as one targeted community.

Despite the widespread use of social networking sites, governments, which control national communication technologies and practice Internet penetra-tion policies, often block completely or censor areas of these popular applica-tions, citing as their justification that the sites violate norms and customs of local culture. There are varying trends with regard to the regulation of these sites, as evident not only in censorship policies, but also in the opening of sites in response to popular protest that fills newspapers and chat rooms. Likewise, the governments block new forms of voice over IP communications, such as Skype and Gizmo, that were available until recent years.

SOCIAL RELATIONS

Individual life cycles revolve around family and social roles much more than friends. Major rites of passage—birth, circumcision, marriage, and death—signal new responsibilities and expectations for an individual. As a youngster, a child grows up learning the importance of family and the ways in which men and women are expected to behave in the adult world. Often living with multiple generations, the child witnesses the ways in which families ex-pand with marriage and birth, rather than fragment off into separate nuclear households. However, a young girl knows that after marriage, she will leave her natal family to join her husband's household. Likewise, boys know that the bride they take must also fit into the daily rhythm of their families since the possibility is great that they will live with the boys' parents and perhaps grandparents. Respect and reverence for the elderly continues, with recogni-tion of their experiences, sacrifices, and knowledge, especially about the times before the oil boom. Most people recognize that the security elderly people once enjoyed—living with family, having needs met—can no longer be taken for granted in today's world, where community and family structures change in response to modernization. Increasingly, elderly people live alone or find themselves isolated from friends and family. As more and more families opt for nuclear households and as traditional neighborhoods dissolve into contempo-rary housing communities, whose responsibility the elderly are and how they will be cared for remain unanswered questions.

Changing family structures raise other concerns about the types of social interactions in which people engage on a daily level. Many Gulf families employ a host of domestic servants, ranging from maids and cooks to drivers and houseboys; some families also employ Westerners as tutors for their children. Initially introduced to offset the burdens of daily life, some now question what is the long-range effect on society when children are raised by nannies who speak other languages, prepare foreign food dishes, and raise children outside local traditions. In places like Dubai, people ask how the city reflects Emirati (yet alone Muslim) values and ways of life, given the presence of foreign workers. It is unclear what direction Gulf populations will take as they sort through complex identity issues that result from changing social relations and new social groups.

HOSPITALITY AND VISITING

Hospitality stands out as a key value in Arab Gulf life, especially among Bedouin, who are known for extending a welcome even to foreign travelers. Traditionally, on greeting a traveler who passed his tent, a Bedouin would provide coffee, food, and shelter for a period of up to three days. At the very least, a guest was expected to drink three small cups of coffee before signaling that he was finished and embarking on the real reason for the visit. It was quite common for hosts to bring out their best offerings in an attempt to make guests feel both welcomed and honored. Folklore tells stories of Bedouin who, in providing a plentiful meal for guests, deprived themselves of their riches and even food. Guests are expected to behave appropriately; accepting the generosity of hosts is paramount. The roots of hospitality stem from the harshness of the desert; providing hospitality gave protection to travelers as well as displayed the honor of the host (and the guest, if he behaved appropriately). Offering entertainment and hospitality is thought to increase a man's honor, and thus his reputation rests on his behavior, rather than his material possessions. Hospitality was, and remains today, a ritualized series of reciprocal behaviors whose set pattern of interactions reinforces the roles and obligations of both host and guest.

Friends and family are expected to visit each other regularly, but especially during holiday periods. Hospitality is even extended to customers in shops, with shopkeepers offering "guests" something to drink and making pleasant conversation. Visiting usually takes place in homes, with men and women entertaining separately. Men will host guests in the home's *majlis*, although sometimes they will also host guests in a restaurant, as well, ordering the food, offering food and drink to guests, and then settling the account. Outside of Oman and Bahrain, a visit to a local's house is unusual, unless one has an intimate or very formal relationship with that individual. Women tend to host more informally and in areas that are either separated from the rest of the house or enclosed without windows. The formal *majlis* or *diwaniya* also has a special role in hospitality. Traditionally, the *majlis* was a meeting place of business where men would discuss social and political issues and where sheikhs would receive kinsmen. Today, *majlis* sessions continue at palaces and other venues that resemble large social clubs, enabling men to voice their concerns with a sheikh, meet others, and engage in conversation. Traditionally, hosts would beckon passing guests to join them, but today, with busy schedules and urban traffic, it is often considered rude to drop in without telephoning first. An exception to this is the formal *majlis* situation that is scheduled and open to all visitors.

A visit often begins with the hosts or a housemaid greeting guests at the door, ushering them into the *majlis,* where plush, upholstered couches and chairs line the walls, oriental carpets grace the floors, and chandeliers dot the ceilings. In homes of lesser wealth, a similar layout unfolds, but one might find couches, mats, and less grand lighting akin to a living room in the West. Guests take seats along the sides of the room, as the head of the room, which features the same furniture, is usually reserved for hosts or especially honored guests. Alongside and in front of each seating area are side tables, where fruits and candies are placed for the guests to sample.

Once the host joins the guests, which can be in a few minutes or after a considerably longer period of time, offerings of cold drinks occur. Usually, water or freshly squeezed fruit juice, which is sometimes combined into elaborate sweet concoctions, is served. Cool drinks not only quell hunger, but also provide refreshment and rehydration. While most Gulf countries permit non-Muslims to apply for an alcohol license and thus consume alcohol for personal usage, alcohol is never served to guests in a Muslim household. Thus many people favor fruit cocktails, serving them to guests as an initial beverage. Following drinks, a variety of other foods are offered such as dates or chocolates; at any time, guests can take from the fresh fruit that usually sits on coffee tables in front of the seating suites. Sometimes cups of tea, flavored with fresh mint and sweetened with sugar, are also offered.

If dinner is not served, coffee service signals the end of the visit. Coffee is a very important element to the visit. Arabic coffee, or *gawhe,* is poured from a highly decorated coffeepot, or *dalla,* into small, demitasse-sized cups without handles, called *finjan*s, and then passed to guests. Unless a guest signals that he has had enough by covering the cup with his hand or, more usually, rocking it back and forth, hosts will continue pouring coffee. Unlike the coffee in other parts of the Middle East, which is thick and dark, Gulf Arabic coffee is thin and amber colored, made from unroasted beans and flavored with cardamom and sometimes saffron. Preparing coffee correctly is considered an art that all members, but especially women, of society are expected to master, as serving coffee is a highly prescribed and expected ritual at nearly all meetings.

The practice of eating from common dishes, or what is often referred to as family style in the West, is popular even at formal meals. However, guests usually do not take their own food, but rather have it served to them by hosts or their household staff. Given the amount of food commonly served, it would be impossible for the guest to finish everything on the plate, and this is not expected of the guest; rather, copious amounts of food reflect Bedouin and local notions of hospitality, with emphasis placed on the amount and variety of foods served. For example, at an elegant meal or one during a holiday celebration, the table or mat might be laid with a lavish spread, with hundreds of dishes that are not unified by a common culinary theme, but rather the offering of hospitality. Gulf meat dishes might sit side by side with Chinese broccoli and beef, French fries, or *sambousas*. Similarly, sweet and savory dishes will be served at the same time, although at the conclusion of the meal, another offering of sweets, along with coffee, will take place.

During a visit, guests and hosts exchange a series of formulaic greetings, after which guests are offered a series of refreshments, including hot and cold beverages, foods, and sweets. Gulf Arabs are very polite and formal, engaging in small talk before other conversations can begin. Commonly, so-called hot conversations, such as those concerning religion or politics, are avoided with guests, although in *majlis* sessions, men might gather to discuss pressing issues or request favors. Inquiring into another's personal life is considered taboo, especially if the questions concern women. When people greet each other, they might ask general questions about the health and well-being of family members but very rarely specific questions about marital relationships, wives, or daughters. Privacy is greatly valued.

Greeting customs vary according to country and context (e.g., in the home or in a business environment), the type of relationship, and the gender of those involved. It is customary on meeting someone to exchange formulaic greetings, which can be quite lengthy. At the very least, one says *"salaam aleykum"* (peace be unto you), to which another answers *"wa aleykum as-salaam"* (and to you peace). Men customarily shake hands, although, in the case of two high-status and close men, they might also rub noses. Men never shake the hand of a woman unless she extends her hand because custom prohibits bodily contact across sexes, except among close family members who cannot potentially serve as marriage partners. Instead, men and women will nod in acknowledgment of each other, and perhaps might exchange a few words. In some cases, people will kiss each other's cheeks a few times; this occurs primarily between close friends and family members. As is customary with Arab populations, people stand very close to one another when greeting each other.

A number of expected and taboo behaviors reinforce the mutuality of visiting. For example, hosts are expected to welcome guests even if it is an inconvenience. Likewise, guests should accept offerings from the host, recognizing the honorable act of hospitality. It is customary to initially refuse an offering such as coffee, but when pressed, the guest is expected to receive whatever is offered even if he or she does not finish it; the play of refusal and acceptance reinforces the gratitude and hospitality associated with the roles of guest and host, respectively. Guests should be careful about the compliments they extend to their hosts because hosts do not expect compliments, as the act of providing is considered honorable unto itself. In addition, a host might feel obligated to give the guest an admired item even if the guest was simply making a passing observation.

FOLKLORE AND FOLK MEDICINE

Gulf Arabs pride themselves on their cultural traditions and folklore, emphasizing the need to disseminate information not only to educate the young, but also to encourage cultural understanding between expatriates and locals. Folklore is literally the ways, beliefs, and crafts of the folk, which in the Gulf context translates to the Bedouin. However, much of the folklore associated with the Bedouin emerges as the foundation of nationalism within the Gulf's recently formed states. Common symbols, such as the falcon or date palm, decorate everything from house gates to government institutions to currency. Heritage centers bring to life key symbols, weaving stories of the past while demonstrating material culture: women weave tents and speak about life in the oasis, while men demonstrate falconry or traditional dances such as the sword dance.

Throughout the major cities of the Gulf states, cultural symbols in the form of public monuments dot major intersections and traffic circles, heralding the heritage of the region. In downtown Doha, next to the site of the new national library, stands a large pillar with a statue of an oryx (a type of gazelle), paying tribute to the state's wildlife and Bedouin past. Omani traffic circles display giant statues of everything from coffeepots and cups, which symbolize Bedouin and Arab hospitality, to Omani-styled chests, which are unique in the region and reflect numerous influences, including the presence of the Portuguese. Both Bahrain and Qatar have pearl monuments in Manama and Doha, respectively. Modern architecture also pays homage to the past through the incorporation of symbolic elements. Numerous buildings are built in the shape of ships, recalling the importance of the sea. In Dubai, the famous Burj al-Arab

(Tower of the Arab) hotel evokes the image of a ship replete with a white sail, while the new Etisalat (the UAE state-owned telecommunications company) building stands with its bow facing a major intersection. Likewise, wind tower motifs are also popular in new construction, branching off from the roofs of houses and other structures. With the convenience of air-conditioning, the wind tower is no longer needed for cooling but is instead used as a decorative architectural element. Many other symbols, including the *khanjar* (dagger), camel, *bukhoor* (incense burner), and *dhow*, enjoy popularity as a reference to tradition.

Pearls occupy a special place in local folklore because of the region's former pearl-diving industry. Pearls are considered items of beauty and value; some people also think pearls have mystical powers for healing or finding a lost love. Pearl diving demanded much strength and fortitude from the divers; they spent large periods of time away from their families, and the job itself was physically tasking. With a stone attached to his foot, a peg attached to his nose, and wax stuffed into his ears, the diver plummeted to the sea bottom, where he quickly filled a basket with shells. After a tug, the diver was then pulled to the surface, where the shells were emptied onto the boat (Gillespie 2006; Seery 1993). The *naham*, or performance leader, led the men in *fidjeri*, or sea-faring songs, particular to pearl divers. Punctuating the rhythmic songs were the drum and hand clapping. The songs provided the divers with motivation as they called out together, singing songs of their toil. People also tell stories about the origin of the pearl. In Bahrain, parents tell their children that a mermaid's teardrop fell into an oyster shell and created the pearl.[1]

Many folkloric traditions revolve around the safety of the individual and especially how to ward off evil spirits, or djinn, from oneself and one's family and community. Taboos and amulets protect those considered especially vulnerable (pregnant women, children, and the sickly). In the UAE, pregnant women wear amulets with verses of the Quran, which is thought to shield them and their unborn children from danger. Moreover, the pregnant woman and some of her family members observe a number of taboos such as avoiding looking at an ugly person or animal, lest the child develop a resemblance; being shielded from bad news; and not walking alone at night unless armed with an iron knife, which is thought to protect against evil (Hurreiz 2002, 86–87). Some groups treat a child for forty days with smoke from *khatf,* a seed that is thought to protect against the evil eye. The belief in spirit possession, or *zar,* is not in accordance with Islam, yet many people continue to believe that spirits can cause harm and take one's soul. Certain places are deemed especially dangerous; Oman's inner mountain area is reputed to be a place where djinn collect the souls of visitors.

Before the twentieth century, modern medicine was quite rare in the Gulf states, and thus people relied on four different types of folk healers: *al-mutabbib* (the traditional healer), *al-'ashshab* (the herbalist), *al-daya* (the midwife), and *al-mutawwa'* (the Muslim religious leader). At other times, others played minor roles. For example, the village barber might perform a circumcision, or other healers might specialize in animals. Everyone was expected to have a general knowledge of herbs and practices for the treatment of common problems such as coughs and diarrhea. However, when more serious ailments arose, it was time to turn to particular kinds of folk healers, who were considered specialists in different areas (Hurreiz 2002, 108).

Two commonly practiced forms of traditional healing were bloodletting (*al-hijama*) and curing by iron (*al-kay*). There are varying forms of bloodletting, from incisions, similar to surgical procedures, to minor procedures, where blood is not forced from the body. In curing by iron, the healer places a hot iron rod next to the afflicted area. This practice has similarities to branding, which is used to mark the ownership of animals (called *al-wasm*). Both bloodletting and curing by iron cured everything from backaches to whooping cough and are considered part of prophetic medicine, a body of literature that details the incorporation of medical practices within Islam (Hurreiz 2002, 108–109). Herbalists used the many available plants and perfumes to cure disease as well as to encourage good health, while midwives attended to gynecological disorders and obstetrics. Religious leaders were consulted for what would be considered problems of the mind and/or soul.

The Calendar

Both the Islamic calendar, which is called the Hijri calendar, and the Gregorian calendar, which is commonly employed in the West, are utilized for scheduling religious and national holidays as well as regulating the business week. Religious and national holidays follow the Islamic calendar, while internationally recognized holidays, such as January 1, adhere to the Gregorian calendar. Throughout the Muslim world, people use the Hijri calendar, which, as a lunar calendar, follows the movement of the moon, rather than the sun, as does the Gregorian calendar. The Hijri calendar begins with Muhammad's emigration from Mecca to Medina, which is commonly thought to have occurred around AD 622. There are twelve lunar months totaling 354 days, eleven days shorter than the Gregorian calendar. Moreover, with a different starting date and length of year, the Hijri calendar does not match up with the Gregorian calendar. A common method for converting the Hijri calendar year to the Gregorian calendar year is to multiply the Hijri year by 0.97 and then add 622.

The twelve months of the Hijri calendar are Muharram, Safar, Rabi' al-awwal, Rabi' al-thani, Jumada al-awwal, Jumada al-thani, Rajab, Sha'aban, Ramadan, Shawwal, Dhu al-Qi'dah, and Dhu al-Hijjah. Unlike the Western calendar, in which days begin at midnight, the first day of the week in the Hijri calendar begins Saturday evening. The seven days of the week are as follows: yom al-ahad, yom al-ithnayn, yom al-thulaathaa', yom al-arbi'aa, yom al-khamis, yom al-jumu'a, and yom al-sabt. Yom al-jumu'a, or gathering day, corresponds to Friday and is the day that Muslims attend sermons at mosques. Holidays are fixed to specific Hijri dates, although often, the exact timing of a holiday, such as Ramadan, is dependent on the sighting of the moon. Consequently, not only do holiday dates vary when compared to a solar calendar— the same holiday will fall on different dates in different years on the Gregorian calendar—but Muslims in neighboring countries might use different start dates for major holidays.

In addition to major religious holidays, each state recognizes a number of international and national days, during which private companies and public institutions close. January 1 is recognized throughout the Gulf, with New Year's Eve celebrations held at private clubs and hotels. National days commemorate the founding of the nation-state, with public heritage displays and other events that celebrate cultural traditions such as falconry, dances, and music. In Oman, it is held on November 18 and is paired with the birthday celebration of His Majesty Sultan Qaboos. Other national days are observed on December 16 (Bahrain), December 2 (UAE), February 25 (Kuwait), and December 18 (Qatar). Kuwait also celebrates Liberation Day (February 26), a happy and sad occasion on which people rejoice for the 1991 liberation yet recognize those fallen in the war; Qatar holds an Independence Day on September 3.

Muslims recognize Friday as a holy day, and thus the workweek in the Gulf is not Monday through Friday with a Saturday-Sunday weekend. Recently, all the Arab Gulf countries, with the exception of Oman, codified the weekend as Friday and Saturday for both public and private sectors; Oman continues to celebrate the weekend on Thursday and Friday. The reasons given for the standardization of the weekend are many, ranging from enabling companies to synchronize more work hours with Western businesses to affording families more shared leisure time. Complicating matters further, the length of the workweek is not standardized. Some companies and institutions work five-day weeks, while others work six- or five-and-a-half-day weeks. Similarly, business hours differ according to industry. Government institutions are usually open until mid-afternoon, although some public sector offices might be open all day or with evening hours. Most private companies work an eight to five or nine to six day. Some businesses work in the morning and the evening, with a break for the midday meal, although this timing is increasingly disappearing as companies shift to a Western-style workday. During Ramadan, companies often observe a six-hour workday. Service establishments, such as malls and grocery stories, open in the early morning and close late at night; some might be open on Friday, but it depends on the country. During the day, when prayer time is announced, music in stores is turned down so that the call to prayer can be heard clearly.

Most individuals who work in nonservice sectors receive significant amounts of vacation, often many weeks, as well as free religious and national holidays from their employers. However, as Islamic holidays are not called until a moon sighting occurs, people are often not given notice of their holiday period until shortly before it occurs; the only exception to this are sanctioned official holidays and celebrations that are fixed to a specific date. As the Gulf countries host a wide variety of religions, many individuals take personal leave to celebrate their holidays. For example, most employers are understanding that expatriates would want to spend Christmas day with family. However, the non-Western calendar complicates life for individuals who are accustomed to Sunday religious services, and thus most churches in the region hold Sunday services on Fridays, the holy day for Muslims. In most countries, Fridays are unique days, on which everything slows down, with retail outlets opening late in the afternoon, long after Friday prayers and lunch have concluded.

During holiday periods, people travel. Not only do a large percentage of the countries have the same holidays (thus facilitating family vacations), but also, the Gulf is a transportation hub to Europe, Asia, Australasia, Africa, and other Gulf countries. It is quite common for airlines and travel companies to feature special Id trips that offer deep discounts to holiday travelers. Individuals and families who do not travel abroad take to the countryside, enjoying themselves with barbeques and family celebrations at beaches, in the mountains, and at other special places such as family farms. Visiting also marks vacation periods, with family and neighbors paying obligatory calls on each other, sharing coffee and sometimes a meal or fieldtrip. Regardless of how one spends his or her holiday period, it is almost always marked by social gatherings that highlight the importance of family relationships within and across nation-state boundaries.

LEISURE ACTIVITIES

Both traditional and modern sports enjoy great popularity among Gulf residents. Falconry, horse racing, and camel racing are the sports of the very wealthy and ruling families since the cost of purchasing, keeping, and training the animals is very high. Sea activities are also popular, as evident by the many boating, *dhow*, and *abra* races. Sporting activities draw both participants and spectators. Karate and basketball attract both men and women, as does soccer, which has a strong following, as people root for their national teams, which compete in local and international matches. When the UAE won the regional soccer title over Oman, men and women alike painted themselves and their cars in national colors, paralyzing the streets with celebrations and elevating the players to the level of celebrities.

The power of the falcon to symbolize Arabia, the desert, and masculinity cannot be overstated. It is commonly associated with the ruling families and the national body and can be found everywhere, painted in national colors on house gates and displayed on currency. Falcon organizations and desert heritage centers organize falconry demonstrations as a means of continuing a tradition that is considered unique to the region. While falconry exhibitions display the abilities of the falcon and its trainer, it was not originally considered a sport; rather, people employed falcons in the desert as a tool for hunting, with hungry families relying on its catch for meat.

Both Saker and Peregrine falcons are used, although the latter are considered more apt for desert hunting because of their speed. A *saggar*, or falcon trainer, works with the bird in developing its ability to track and hunt its prey. Each *saggar* develops a personal relationship with the falcon, naming it and slowly conditioning it to his voice and touch. During training, the falcon wears a leather hood that covers its eyes and is usually tied to a post for a roost. When handling the falcon, *saggar*s wear thick, protective gloves that shield the arm from sharp talons. Once the falcon and *saggar* develop a relationship, the hood is removed so visual contact can be established. Training continues with the *saggar* getting the falcon to respond to his commands and guiding its flight through lures of meat that are raised and lowered. During the actual hunt, the falcon ascends high into the sky, spotting the prey (birds, hares, and other small animals), following it, and then eventually diving to kill the animal either in flight or on the ground. The speed, grace, and diving abilities of the falcon are tremendous, as are the distances it covers during a hunt; men take pride and honor in the abilities of their falcons. Today, hunting parties in SUVs follow the falcon during its flight and pursuit of prey over many miles, replacing the horses that were once used.

The small yet strong Arabian horse is cherished for its grace, speed, and stamina in short-distance sprints and long-distance endurance races. Fetching large sums of money, especially when used for racing or studding, Arabian horses belong primarily to the wealthy. Among sheikhs, the gift of a horse is seen as an appropriate and noble gift. Although most people cannot afford the cost or space needs associated with raising horses, they can enjoy their beauty and agility at the many races held through the winter and spring months.

Throngs of spectators fill the many tracks of grass, sand, and tarmac, watching favored horses capture cups such as the Bahrain Silver Cup or the Dubai World Cup. Islamic law prohibits gambling, but speculating on which horses will place is accepted. An evening at the races can be very inexpensive, with many tracks offering standing-only areas for free or a nominal fee, or an expensive affair where people dine from lavish buffets and watch from enclosed box seats. Whichever route is chosen, horse racing offers a pleasant social environment that also honors the place of the horse in the Arabian past. Another form of racing is the endurance ride. During an endurance race, riders traverse large expanses of desert, riding on the sand course for hours. Most people gather to watch the beginning or conclusion of these races, although some follow along in SUVs, rooting for their favorite rider and horse. Primarily, sheikhs and elites practice this sport, but increasingly, it is gaining popularity among sheikhas of royal families, who hold their own female-only endurance races.

Camels are also used for racing, but they do not draw the same crowds or prize packages. Recently, Gulf camel racing has drawn a large amount of publicity and criticism from international rights groups and the media for its employment of very young boys from south Asia as jockeys. Often, these children were raised from an early age with the sole purpose of riding camels, and thus allegations were levied that in the process, the well-being of the boys was not ensured. Today, small robots have replaced human riders. Regulated via remote control, these small robots, perched atop the camel's back, slightly behind its hump, kick and whip the camel as the animal's owner follows alongside in a truck or SUV. Camels need less directional guiding than horses, and thus the robots are seen as a humane solution to the utilization of child jockeys. At the camel tracks, the excitement is palpable, with the camels running in a fast, long-legged gait and spectators following outside the track in their SUVS. The environment around camel racing also attracts onlookers, who watch the camels as they are turned out for exercise (here they are ridden by humans), bedecked in colorful bridles, blankets, and other decorations.

The Gulf coastline affords numerous miles of seafront for beach activities, picnics, bathing, and boating. Women rarely go to public beaches because to be seen publicly in beach attire would violate cultural norms of modesty; rather, when bathing, they often favor women-only environments, or if they are with family at the beach, especially in conservative communities such as Oman, they will often go into the water fully clothed in their *abayas*. Men, on the other hand, visit beaches with their children, swimming and playing with them in the sand. When wives accompany their families on these outings, they often stay in the shade, watching their families and partaking in other activities. Some people might fish, but it is generally not considered a leisure activity. Traditional fishing, especially in Kuwait and Bahrain, uses traps and

Camels out for exercise near a racetrack, Camel City outside Doha, Qatar. Courtesy of Anders Linde-Laursen.

a series of netted poles that are pounded into the sand along the shoreline and then extended into the sea. The fish become trapped in a series of narrowing enclosures as they follow high tide; afterward, the fishermen can easily pull them from the traps during low tide.

While not a sport, shopping and spending time meandering around the numerous malls are taken to new levels in Gulf communities. Except for winter, the Gulf's climate offers little respite from heat and humidity, and thus many activities move indoors. Malls offer spas, child play areas, skating rinks, shallow-bottomed boating, and in Dubai, a kilometer-long ski slope. Family and friends will spend a day at the mall, eating in the numerous restaurants, window shopping, and walking the corridors as if they were taking a stroll in their neighborhood. It is not surprising, then, that new malls construct their corridors in ways that suggest city streets and environments. For those with an urge to buy, the Dubai Shopping Festival occurs annually, drawing tens of thousands of visitors from across the Gulf for a monthlong extravaganza of sales, performance, and amusement activities.

For those interested in outdoor activities, desert excursions offer the possibility of staying in the desert overnight, enjoying the clear skies and quietness of its expanse. In Qatar and the UAE, families often keep so-called farms, which are more like rural homes, for weekend trips out of the city. People consider these excursions as essential parts of daily life, citing that they help people reconnect with the desert environments of their ancestors. For those without second houses, adventure companies offer everything from dune bashing, where SUVs ride up and down large sand dunes, to dune boarding, where skiers ride dunes on snowboards. Often, an evening barbeque with traditional foods and music follows a day in the desert.

Despite the popularity of video games, amusement parks, movies, and sports, many Gulf children continue to play traditional games. In Bahrain, girls might play *al-shaqhah*, a game in which young girls jump over each other's hands and feet. In Qatar, children will play *umm al-lal,* with one girl playing the role of a mother defending her children against a wolf. Young boys in Qatar or the UAE might play *al-ghomaid,* a version of blindman's bluff, in which one child is blindfolded and must catch one of the other children, who call out to him, or may play with small boats (*al-lomsabaq* in Bahrain and *hawari* in the UAE). Other games include playing with marbles or spinning tops, seeking buried treasure, or challenging each other to a game of hide-and-seek. While many games are sex-specific, some games, such as *al-khaishaisheh* (hide-and-seek), are played by both sexes.[2]

NOTES

1. See http://www.everyculture.com.
2. See http://www.everyculture.com.

8

Music and Dance

WITHIN THE ARAB Gulf region, traditional music and dance represent the interplay between lives lived out in the desert and on the sea, between indigenous and foreign traditions, and between Arab Islamic cultural life and the cultural life of Persia, India, and eastern Africa (Hurreiz 2002). Music and dance are intimately connected, as are music and poetry. Dance and music were part of the fabric of people's lives: lullabies, children's songs, work songs, wedding songs, and songs for religious rituals. In terms of contributions to world music traditions, the Arab Gulf region unites traditional Arab Bedouin music with the musical heritages of eastern Africa, Iran, and India—regions connected to the Gulf through trade—in a rich, distinctive musical style known as Khaleeji. Khaleeji music is marked by its pentatonic (five-tone) scales and 6/8 rhythms. This music of the cities emphasizes the oud, drums, and hand clapping. This style has become so popular that singers from other Arab countries have incorporated Khaleeji songs into their repertoires, and there are radio stations in the region that broadcast only this style of music.

MUSIC

Instruments

What makes Gulf music distinctive is the instruments used to perform it. These instruments belong to the string, wind, and percussion/rhythm families. The following discussion applies most closely to the instruments used in Omani musical traditions, although instruments such as the *rababa*, the oud, various drums and cymbals, and flutes are found throughout the region. Ordinary household items, such as water jars and grain or coffee mortars, were also used as percussion instruments in the pearl-diving songs. Different patterns of hand clapping also figure in this musical genre (Lambert 1998, 651).

In Oman, the string family instruments are the *rababa,* the *tanbura,* and the oud. The *rababa* is the traditional one-stringed fiddle that is played in a vertical position, resting on the musician's thigh. The *rababa* was used as accompaniment to a poet reciting or singing his poetry. It is fretless and can produce four or five tones easily on its neck, without having to move the left hand much.

The *tanbura* has remained largely unchanged since its first appearance about 2700 BC in Sumer. It is a six-stringed lyre, with the sixth and first strings positioned closely together. The sixth string plays the suboctave of the highest note; its placement next to the first string allows the musician to reach all six strings at once. The instrument is played by positioning the left hand behind the strings, where it is used to mute all the strings except the one playing the melody. The strings are beaten with a horn (usually the end of a bull's horn). This instrument is found throughout the Middle East and in Egypt and Africa (the Nubian area of Sudan).

The oud is a pear-shaped, fretless stringed instrument played with a pick, a predecessor to the Western lute. It, too, is an ancient instrument; one is pictured on a cylinder seal from Mesopotamia that dates back 5,000 years ago. The modern instrument consists of eleven strings arranged in five pairs of two strings, with the lowest, the eleventh, a singleton. The back of the instrument is bowl-like (rather than flat, like a guitar), which allows the instrument to resonate.

The wind family includes the *mizmar,* the *zamr,* the *qasaba,* and the *habban.* The *mizmar* is a double-reed wooden instrument. Playing it requires that the musician blow strongly and without interruption. The player will store air in his cheeks (inflating them) and breathe through his nose. Skilled players can blow for several hours without stopping. The *zamr* is made from bamboo and consists of two parallel pipes of equal length bound together, with the reed cut into the body of the pipe. The instrument can have five, six, or seven holes, although the five-holed variant is the most common. The *qasaba* is a single cylindrical pipe made of bamboo, wood, or metal, with no mouthpiece and open at both ends—similar to the *nai.* It has six holes in the front and one in the back. The musician plays it by blowing sideways into one of the openings. The *habban* (Scottish bagpipe) is a modern introduction into the region. The instrument in Oman has both drone and melodic pipes, while the version used in Bahrain and Qatar has double pipes playing the melody and no drone pipes.

The percussion/rhythm family includes many different forms of double-skinned and single-skinned drums as well as other rhythm instruments that are shaken, beaten, or blown. The double-skinned drums include the *rahmani* drums, the *ranna*, the *kasir* drums, and the *mirwas*. These drums can be tuned by tightening the ropes that lash the skins to the body of the drum. The drums may be beaten by sticks on both sides, by a stick on one side and a hand on the other, or by hands on both sides. The *rahmani* has a deep, full sound suitable to its function of providing the main rhythmic base for the music. The *kasir*, by contrast, has a higher-pitched sound and is used for embellishment and ornamentation. The *rahmani tawil* (long rahmani) has an even heavier sound. It is usually carried vertically and beaten on one side only. The *ranna* fills the middle between the *rahmani* and *kasir*. There are two other variants of the *kasir*: the *kasir qasir* (short *kasir*) and the *kasir mufaltah* (flat *kasir*). These are usually beaten by sticks, although the short *kasir* may be beaten with both hands. The *mirwas* is the smallest of the drums. The player holds it with one hand and strikes it with the other; sometimes the index finger of the holding hand is used to play lightly along to fill out the rhythm.

The single-skinned drums consist of various forms of the *musundu*, the *duff*, and the *baz*. The *musundu* drums originated in Africa and are used in musical traditions that came out of the connections between Oman and the eastern African coasts. A single skin is fitted to a long conical body made of a hollowed piece of wood or wood strips that have been glued together into a cone shape. The player controls the drum's tightness either by heating it or by rubbing a special paste of kneaded dates, grease, and ashes into the skin. Some forms of the drum are tied to the musician's waist by a belt and played with both hands, with the drum between the player's legs like a hobby horse. Other forms of the drum rest on the ground and are played either seated or standing, depending on the height of the drum.

The *duff* drums consist of round wooden frames of different sizes, with one side covered by a skin; bells and copper cymbals may also be incorporated into the wooden frame. The player holds the drum with one hand in front of his chest and beats it with the palm of his other hand. The body of the *baz* class of drums looks like a bowl that has been covered by a skin. This drum, known as the *quta*, has the skin fixed onto the bowl shape by ropes placed around the body of the drum. If the body of the drum is clay or metal, the skin may be directly fastened onto the body. The drum is beaten with a piece of rubber or a thin stick.

Other rhythmic instruments include various forms of rattles that are shaken by hand, or worn on the legs or body and shaken by movements. The *khirkhasha* is a rattle with a round metal body with a handle that is filled with small, dry grains, stones, or beads. The *mangur* is a wide belt of cloth to which hundreds of sheep hooves are sewn closely together. The player ties the belt on and plays it by moving his hips. The *khirkash* is composed of bells tied to a sash, worn around the waist of a male dancer who varies the sound by the movements of his body. Men may also wear a *khalakhil,* a wooden rattle worn around the ankles. Women may wear the *lubus,* small bells tied on a rope and worn around the ankle, or the *adad,* round bangles made of silver and filled with dry grain or stones. Rounding out these instruments are cymbals (*sihal*), sea shells that are blown or struck together, empty tin containers that have been squeezed together and are played with two sticks, and an oryx, ibex, or buffalo horn that is blown to produce a single tone.

Sung Poetry

One of the earliest forms of musical expression is this region would have been sung poetry, the heart and emblem of Bedouin culture (Jargy 1998). From the earliest times, poetry and song were closely linked. The poet would accompany his performance with the *rababa,* while group recitals might also use various forms of drums. The sung poetry consisted of three main types: *al-hijni,* which began as camel riders' music (with a rhythm that mimicked a camel's gait) but later came to resemble warriors' songs; *al-'arda,* warriors' songs; and *al-samiri,* love songs.

Two lines of ten to twenty performers kneel facing each other in the sand to perform *al-samiri* singing, leaving space between them for the dancers. Frame drums, double-skinned drums, and hand clapping provide the rhythmic accompaniment. One line drums and sings, while the other answers and moves their shoulders while kneeling. In the Gulf, the bands are often professionals, with their group names painted on their instruments. The *al-arda* gathers all the men of a tribe or village to perform. Two rows of dancers stand in a semicircle, waving swords and serving as the chorus. The poets singing stand between the two lines; their verses extol the honor of the tribe.

Sung poetry was passed orally from master to pupil over the generations. Modern singers have learned these songs from family members. Improvisation has always been part of the process of transmission. The original creator of the songs, the *sha'ir,* needed another person for his songs to live on: the memorizer, the *rawi,* or bard. When the *rawi* would reperform the work of the *sha'ir,* he might add his own improvisations or polish the poetry he was singing. In this way, the songs were continually being adapted to their changing environments. Jargy (1998) notes that no system of musical or textual notation can capture the subtleties of the actual performances themselves. In this way, he sees this genre of music as representing a communal possession, rather than works belonging to an individual, known author.

Pearling Songs

Just as this sung poetry was rooted in the nomadic life of the Bedouin tribes of the region, other forms of work produced their own song traditions. Along the coasts in Bahrain, Kuwait, Qatar, and Oman, there was a rich heritage of music connected to life on ships: the merchant trading vessels and the pearl-diving vessels.[1] There were songs sung while loading and unloading cargo, songs for raising the masts, and songs to help with rowing. Each pearl-diving ship had a singer, the *nahham*, who would encourage the crew to work hard during the day and would entertain them as they returned home in the evening. The songs for working had short, rhythmic cycles, while the entertainment songs, known as *fijiri* (until dawn), were long and drew on legends for their lyrics. Women, gathered on the seashore waiting for the ships to return, would sing their own songs begging the sea to let the men return safely and describing the difficulties of life as a pearler. Women also sang in small groups as they did their own work—songs for grinding wheat, for fetching wood, and for cooking *hareis* and lullabies for babies and young children.

Sawt and Other Forms

Besides these work songs, the Arab Gulf states are also known for urban forms of music, such as the *sawt*, the Arabic blues genre influenced by African, Indian, and Persian music and centered in Kuwait and Bahrain.[2] In this musical genre, the singer is accompanied by the oud, a short-necked lute; hand clapping; and a double-skinned drum. The dance that accompanies the song cycle is known as the *zafan*; its characteristic movements are sudden leaps and kneeling down. Lyrics are drawn from classical Arabic poetry as well as colloquial poetry, mainly from Yemen. *Sawt* was first recorded in 1927 in Iraq and in 1929 in Cairo. The cycle consists of a prelude played by the instruments, a short introductory poem sung in free rhythm, the *sawt* itself, and a short concluding poem sung to a conventional melody. As a genre, it has roots both in classical Arab music and in popular, oral traditions. Some of the more well-known performers include Shadi al-Khaleej, Nabil Shaeil, and Abdullah El Ruisheed (Kuwait) and Khalid al-Shaikh and Sultan Hamid (Bahrain).

In Oman, one additional musical form is found performed by men who are descendants of slaves brought from Africa. The *lewa* groups use the *musundu* drums, conch trumpets, and canisters, on which they drum. The group also includes a *zammar*, who plays the *mizmar*. The musicians arrange themselves in a circle, except for the *zammar*, who paces in the center as he plays. The *zammar* starts the song and plays slowly for a number of minutes, then the drummers join in and the pace of the music gradually increases. The musicians play for three named dances, singing songs in Swahili and Arabic about Africa and seafaring. It is not uncommon for performances to produce trances in the dancers.

Women's Music

Women's singing has always been acceptable within Islam, although it is debated in parts of Arabia today. There are anecdotes about the Prophet's life in which he looked with favor on women singing. In Qatar, women and girls used to participate in a form of public performance, called *al-moradah*, in the week before the Ids (Abu Saud 1984). They would go into the desert away from the men so they could sing and dance without being seen. Young girls aged thirteen to fifteen would stand in two lines facing each other to dance and sing. One line would sing a verse, and the other would repeat it. Their songs reflected what was happening in society at the time. They sang about love and marriage, beauty and good manners, and if at war, war songs. Women of all social classes, dressed in their finest clothing, took part in the event. Mothers of sons would check out the young women to see if they could find a suitable bride among them. This event was abandoned in the 1950s, after it became clear that the young men would not leave the women alone. In one incident, a young man drove his car between the two lines of singing girls.

Most professional female musicians perform folk music, although a few very famous singers have crossed over to more public art performances. It is possible to hear women's folk music on the radio, see it performed on television, and attend live performances in Kuwait, Qatar, Bahrain, and the United Arab Emirates (UAE; Campbell 1998). Professional female musicians may perform for all-female audiences at wedding celebrations or religious ceremonies. Women may also perform as part of mixed, male-female folk music groups; these groups often perform for private parties. In addition to these folk music groups, some women perform the *sawt* song cycles for private parties in people's homes. These performers are more skilled, and their dress, jewelry, and hairstyles will be more elaborate, than those of the women in the folk music groups. In Sohar in Oman, all professional female musicians are descendents of slaves.

Besides singing to infants and young children, one of the major occasions for women to perform occurs at weddings. The group of musicians, the *firqa*, is organized around a well-known woman singer, the *mutriba*, after whom the group is named. The *mutriba* is usually the most gifted musician in the group, who sings and may play oud as well. The other group members will play different types of drums and the tambourine and will serve as the chorus singers. When the musicians arrive at the wedding, they will begin to set up their instruments and sound equipment and tune drums (by heating them) and instruments. The *mutriba* begins the melody and the different drums gradually come in. Once the entire group is playing, the audience will join in with singing, clapping, and the *zagharit* ululation. Most of the songs that the women perform focus on love, marriage, and weddings. Usually, the songs consist of several verses and a refrain, broken by instrumental interludes.

Traditionally, women's patronage was essential for a woman's group to gain an audience. Performing at highly visible women's occasions, such as women's charity events, and referrals from prominent women would help a group gain prestige. Where women's music is broadcast on radio and television, such private patronage is no longer as essential for women's groups to be successful. In addition, governments in the region have begun to support the preservation of their musical traditions by creating institutes to study music and folklore (such as the Oman Centre for Traditional Music[3]) as well as sponsoring national performing groups or sending folk music groups to represent the country at international festivals. In Qatar, some folk music groups receive a monthly salary from the Department of Culture and Arts of the Ministry of Information. Women's groups from the region thus can develop a broader, regional audience for their performances. With electronic recording technology more available, cassette and compact disk recordings now circulate, as well.

Several female performers have crossed over to become recording stars in their own right. Ahlam Ali al-Shamsi was one of the first to achieve fame as a singing star. Born in Bahrain, she started singing as a child at weddings and religious ceremonies. Discovered by Kuwaiti music composer Anwar Abdullah, she began to make recordings with a local Gulf music production company, Funoon al-Emarat. She became a citizen of the UAE in 1996. She has brought out multiple albums and has her own fan Web site.[4] Hind, also born in Bahrain, was discovered by Anwar Abdullah while studying at the university, which she left to begin her musical career. She married in 2002 and was a mother in 2003, but by 2004, she was divorced. In 2005, she signed with the music production company Rotana, which released her album in 2005, which relaunched her career. She, too, has her own fan Web site.[5]

Contemporary Music

Besides its folk music traditions, classical Arab music has also been supported by Gulf governments. In 1997, the Bahrain Orchestra for Arabic Music was formed. From a small beginning, the orchestra grew in size and added choral elements. The orchestra has played with Bahraini and Gulf singers, has performed traditional music, and has debuted the work of modern Bahraini composers such as Majeed Marhoon. The Royal Oman Symphony Orchestra was founded in 1985 by order of Sultan Qaboos. The orchestra consists of all local musicians, trained in Western musical traditions by foreign teachers.

Originally, the orchestra was all male, but since 1988, female musicians have also been recruited. The orchestra has a regular performance schedule in Oman and also travels to international competitions. Composer Lalo Schifrin was commissioned to compose a piece for the orchestra and produced *Symphonic Impressions of Oman*, which he recorded with the London Symphony Orchestra. In the UAE, the UAE Philharmonic Orchestra was able to begin offering a regular Symphony Series in 2007 after sixteen months of development under director Philip Maier. In 2007, the Qatar Foundation, established by the emir, announced that it would create the Qatar Symphony Orchestra, to unite classical Arabic music with classical Western music.

The Gulf region is also home to more modern musical traditions. The originator of the hip-hop music scene in Bahrain was a producer named DJ Outlaw (Mohammed Ghuloom). He is currently recording what will be the country's first hip-hop and rhythm and blues compilation. In 2003, he pulled together the first rap band in Bahrain, a group named Infinity. Bahrain also produced the progressive rock band Osiris, which has been playing since the 1980s and has achieved some international recognition. Dubai is a regular stop for Western rock musicians, and the number of rock concerts featuring prominent Western talent has continued to grow. Dubai has been home, as well, to an International Jazz Festival.

Recordings and Preservation

Researchers made the first field recordings in the region in 1909, which are now stored in Leiden (Campbell 1998, 38). The first commercial recordings were made in the 1920s and early 1930s.[6] *Sawt* dominated the Gulf music scene in the 1950s and 1960s. In recent years, Gulf governments have actively worked to preserve their own folk traditions through establishing folklore institutes such as found in Qatar and Oman. Folk music is featured on radio and television programming in all Gulf countries.

DANCE

There is no clear ruling within Islam about whether dancing is permitted or prohibited, so different groups of Muslims have developed their own beliefs about whether to allow dancing. For some, dancing is strictly forbidden, not because there is anything sinful in dancing itself, but because it might create an atmosphere that would lead people to sin. For others, as long as dancing is done in single-sex settings, it is permitted. For still others, watching professional dancers is permissible, but the watchers themselves would not dance. Finally, for some Muslims, dance (and music) are integral parts of their worship practices and help bring them closer to Allah. On the Arabian Peninsula, traditional folk dance was an important part of social life in both tribes and villages. People danced to celebrate major life events, as part of religious holidays, and as part of their work routine. Islam could not stamp out those traditions.

In the Arab Gulf states, some dances are performed only by men or only by women. Many other dances are done by both men and women. Where space is available, men and women are segregated so that men dance in male spaces for male audiences and women dance in female spaces for female audiences. Whether the dancers are segregated into separate spaces or separate lines is a function of location and level of religiosity; people living in urban areas and families that are more conservative are more likely to use separate spaces (Adra 1998, 704).

Most dancing is done in line formations, with the dancers judged by how well they move in unison. Besides lines, dancers may use square, circle, or semicircle formations. Some fishing or pearling community dances are done kneeling or sitting, as if on a ship. Common steps and movements include running steps, step-hops, step-together-step hops, and step-together-step-steps, with a turn on the last step or hop. Leaps, knee bends, and vertical jumping punctuate the dances (Adra 1998, 704). Within these patterns, dancers improvise. Gulf women have a unique movement that involves swinging the head with hair loose while holding their right hand on their upper chest, a movement known as *na'ash, tanawush,* or *nuwwash.*[7] Women's social dancing, done wearing a long, loose-fitting robe known as a *thoub,* uses movements of the hands meant to show off the garment. Men may hold daggers, swords, or poles that they wave while dancing. Dances can be classified into warfare dances, work-related dances, "foreign" dances, women's dances for weddings and other entertainments, *zar* healing rituals, and Sufi religious dances.

Dances of Warfare

Exhibition dances are often performed by men only. The most common are those connected to warfare, the genre known as *al-'arda* (also known as *al-'ayyala* in the UAE or *al-razha* in Oman). This dance portrays a mock battle. The dancers stand in two rows, facing each other. In the UAE, men stand close together with hands around each other's waists, creating a strong front. Drummers and swordsmen move around in the space between the dancing men, advancing and retreating before the lines of men. A group of young girls joins the dance, swinging their hair from side to side in *na'ash,* reminding the men of their obligation to protect the women. In Qatar, the two rows of men wave sticks or swords as they dance. In the UAE, there are two regional variants of this genre, known as *al-harbiyya* and *al-wahhabiyya.* In the first, the dance is performed to singing only, and the songs control the dancers' movements.

Cane dance, Bab al Shams resort, Dubai, UAE. Courtesy of Anders Linde-Laursen.

In the second, performed in rural areas and coastal villages of Ras al-Khaimah and al-Fujayrah, the men are arranged in rows and carry weapons such as sticks, swords, or guns with sticks. They raise and lower their weapons in unison, as they dance to the rhythm of the drums. It is a slow, dignified male dance, and no women participate (Hurreiz 2002). In Oman, the 'ayyala features two rows of men armed with sticks or swords who face each other, move forward, and withdraw, as their heads make a back-and-forth movement reminiscent of the head of a walking camel (Lambert 1998, 654). These dances are often performed at national celebrations, as political leaders dance side by side with ordinary citizens; at wedding celebrations; for state visits; and even at football games. They are accompanied by songs that speak of tribal honor and male bravery (Adra 1998, 707).

In Oman, the *razha* is a men's dance performed using swords. The dancers leap into the air and must land firmly. Swords are also thrown into the air and caught. *Razha al-Kabira* is today used to celebrate Sultan Qaboos. The dancers "attack" each other using slow movements and attempt to hit their opponents on the left thumb. In the Dhofar region, men dance the *bar'aa*. Two men, each holding a dagger in his right hand and his *shal* (a piece of cloth worn around the waist to hold the dagger) in his left hand, retreat and advance, while leaping into the air on one foot in the characteristic move of the dance. As he retreats and advances, each makes a full circle.

While women had either no part or a minor part in men's war dances, there was one traditional dance involving attacks that was performed by women. In Kuwait and coastal towns along the Gulf, *al-fareesa* (also *farisa*) was a dance performed by women, disguised as men, for certain national and religious holidays. A woman wearing traditional men's clothing would enter with a box in the shape of a horse hanging off her shoulders. She would be joined by two other women, also wearing men's clothing, one of whom carried a sword and the other a spindle. The horsewoman would dance forward and backward and move around as if to avoid the attacks of the other two dancers. The swordswoman would try to "kill" the horsewoman.

Work-Related Dances

Work-related dances included dances related to going to sea as well as dances drawn from the seasonal round of farming. Dance movements mimicked how people performed their work tasks, or work movements were turned into dances. In Bahrain, farm workers thresh wheat in a dance of sorts, circling the pile and beating it with sticks, all in a definite rhythm. Pounding wheat to make *hareis* (a porridge of pounded wheat, butter, meat, and spices) in Bahrain and Qatar takes on that same sort of rhythmic movement. Clearly, this made the work more efficient and helped people to cope with the boredom of what were otherwise tedious, repetitive tasks.

Pearl divers throughout the region had a rich heritage of both music and dance to accompany their work. As the ships were being readied to go to sea, a mournful dance known as *al-sikini* was performed, accompanied by hand clapping and reed instruments (Adra 1998, 708). On board the ship, the *fijiri* occupied the men's evenings. Kneeling in lines, they would rhythmically slap the deck with their hands, then use hand and arm movements to come to a sitting position, before beginning again. Additional dances were done for pulling up anchor and to celebrate the return to shore.

Foreign Dances

In the UAE, there were several dances that were viewed as "foreign" dances—*al-lewa* (of African origin, also performed in Oman) and *al-habban* (of Persian origin). There is less concern with segregation of men and women in these dances, possibly because of their foreign origins. Because these dances may be mixed, they are often frowned on by devout Muslims. Tradition has it that Omani merchants brought *al-lewa* to the UAE. The dance is performed for weddings and other major celebrations. The dancers are accompanied by drummers and a *mizmar* player, who moves around in the center of the circle or semicircle that the dancers form around the musicians. The dance consists of two step-touches forward followed by two step-touches backward, twisting in a counterclockwise fashion.[8] Men dance in one circle, with women in another. The dance is very relaxed and can go on for hours.

The dance known as *al-habban* (also called *al-hubban*) takes its name from the main instrument played, a goatskin bagpipe. Here, again, men and women dance in separate lines, facing each other, with the musicians between them. As the men retreat two steps, the women advance, and then the pattern is reversed, with women retreating and men advancing. They continue until the song is completed and then take two steps sideways. What follows is a duet of sorts between the drummer and a couple between the lines. The woman twirls, holding handkerchiefs in her hands, while the man moves in a rocking motion (Adra 1998, 710).

Women's Dances

Women dance for weddings, for other community celebrations, and for entertainment. In Qatar and Oman, *al-murada* is a women's line dance. The women stand shoulder to shoulder, holding hands in two lines. The women sing as they step forward and back; after completing several verses, the two lines take turns moving forward to meet the other line and retreating as the other line advances in turn. In Kuwait and Qatar, women perform *al-khamery* or *al-sameri* at weddings. The first dance involves a single, cloaked dancer who bends over, straightens up, and moves backward, while shimmying her shoulders. Dancers wearing *thoubs*, the long, elaborately embroidered robes, cover half their faces with the robe and move forward and backward, while shaking their hips. Turning, the dancer uncovers her face and performs *na'ash*, shaking her hair to the music. In Oman, a widely performed dance is the *raqs al-nisaa*, performed by two women at a time, who move among the sitting women, holding their veils and taking small, measured steps.[9] In the Ibri region, women dance *al-wailah*. The women place their right hands on the shoulders of the women next to them and begin to move around in unison. Each dancer holds a rattle in her free hand; the leader of the dance uses her rattle to signal when the women should change places in a circle.

The *Zar* and Sufi Dancing

When an individual is believed to be possessed by spirits, the healing ritual of the *zar* will be performed to exorcise the spirits. In the Gulf region, the dance performed is known as *al-nuban* (after Nubia, from which the dance is said to have spread to the Gulf more than 150 years ago). The ritual combines drumming, singing, and dancing. The dancers wear belts hung with goats' hooves, and as they stamp their feet, the belts rattle, adding to the rhythm. Men and women participate in the dance. They form two lines facing each other. The lines of dancers retreat from or advance on each other. *Zar* music gradually builds to a climax, with the drummers drumming faster and faster. Dancers often enter into trance states.

Sufism represents the mystical dimension of Islam. Sufis believe that it is possible for them to experience union with God while still alive. Individuals attach themselves to a master, who teaches through allegory, parable, and metaphor (as well as personal example). To lose their sense of self and approach God, Sufis often perform devotional dancing along with the repetition of the names of God. Swaying back and forth, leaping, and whirling all allow the dancer to reach a trance state.

Western Dance Traditions in the Gulf

Western dance traditions, such as ballet, entered the Middle East only very recently. The first ballet school in Egypt opened in 1958, while Algeria's school was started in 1970. The Iraqi Institute is the oldest in the region. There are no official ballet troupes in the Gulf states. As with classical Western music, troupes are brought in from Russia, Europe, or the United States to perform for Gulf citizens. When the Hungarian Donetsk Group performed the ballet *Queen of Sheba* in Oman, the dancers wore costumes that covered their legs in deference to Oman's conservative religious culture. Expatriates (and locals) in the region, however, can study a variety of Western dance forms, such as ballet, modern dance, or Irish step dancing, or even classical Indian dance, at numerous private dance studios operating in the major urban cities.

NOTES

1. Examples of these songs can be found at http://www.zeryab.com/E/index.htm under the link for "Bahri" music. All files require RealPlayer.

2. Examples of these songs can be found at http://www.zeryab.com/E/index.htm under the link for "Aswat" music, for examples from Kuwait, and the link for "Bahraini" music, for examples from Bahrain. All files require RealPlayer.

3. See http://www.octm-folk.gov.om/meng/default.asp.

4. See http://www.ahlamvoice.ws/main/intro.htm.

5. See http://www.hindworld.com/.

6. A number of commercial recordings of Gulf music are available. The Gallo label has produced a four-volume set, recorded by Simon Jargy and Poul Røvsing Olsen, titled *A Musical Anthology of the Arabian Peninsula*. Volume 1 is sung poetry, volume 2 is pearl-diving music, volume 3 is *sawt*, and volume 4 is women's songs. Another collection is called *Music from the Arabian Gulf*. There are two collections of traditional music from Oman, a collection of *fidjeri* from Bahrain, and a collection of *sawt* from

Kuwait. A number of other albums featuring individual Gulf artists can be found at the Maqam Web site, http://www.maqam.com/arabicmusic_arabiangulf.html, which specializes in the music, film, and instruments of the Middle East, Mediterranean, and India.

7. An example of an American dance group performing a Gulf Khaleeji-style dance that includes *na'ash* (choreographed by Kay Hardy Campbell, a researcher of Gulf music and dance) can be seen at http://www.jawaahir.org/images/Video/Henna%2008% 20Halaa%20excerpt%20sm.wmv.

8. An example of *lewa* can be seen at http://www.youtube.com/watch?v= PP55Fk6zH6U&feature=related.

9. See discussion at the Web site of the Ministry of Information for the Sultanate of Oman, http://www.omanet.om/english/culture/folk_song.asp?cat=cult.

Glossary

abaya   Cloaklike garment worn by women that is often black and worn over clothing.

abd   "Slave"; used to denote ethnic heritage category in some Gulf states.

aflaj   Traditional irrigation system that channels water from streams, springs, and wadis.

Ajam   "Persian"; used to denote the ethnic category of those who came from Iran.

al-nabati   Poetic (in vernacular Arabic) adaptation of traditional poems that are sung in shorter forms.

badqeer   Wall ventilation system that pulls air and circulates it within a building.

barjeel   Wind tower ventilation system that captures breezes, funneling them into buildings.

burj   Tower.

burqa   Traditional mask worn on the face, primarily by Bedouin and older women.

dhow   Category of traditional boats used for fishing and trade.

dishdasha   Male full-length, dresslike garment that is often white or cream colored.

diwaniya   Meeting place of business, now used to signify a parlor room.

djinn   Spirits often perceived as evil.

falaj   Plural of *aflaj*.

freej   Traditional neighborhood, also the name of a popular animated television series.

Fusha   Classical form of Arabic that differs from vernacular Arabic or Khaleeji and that is spoken in the Gulf.

ghutra   Square cloth that is folded and worn over the head by men, often in white or colored checkered designs.

hadar   Settled people who are traders, often of Bedouin descent.

Hadith   Sayings of the Prophet that are transmitted as a guide for how to live one's life.

hajj   Pilgrimage, often but not exclusively used to denote pilgrimage to Mecca; also one of the pillars of Islam.

halal   Literally, "permissible," but usually used with reference to how animals are slaughtered.

haram   Word used to reference anything forbidden; opposite of *halal*.

hijab   Head covering worn by women over the hair, neck, and shoulders.

Hijri calendar   Islamic lunar calendar.

Ibadi   Sect of Islam originating from Kharajite rebellion against the fourth caliph and emphasizing the distinction between moral and immoral leadership.

ijma   Scholarly consensus over the meaning of elements in the Quran and Hadith.

ijtihad   Independent reasoning within legal (Sharia) decisions.

ikhwan   Holy warriors within Wahhabism.

imam   Religious leader who knows the hidden and true meaning of the Quran.

Ismaili   Sect of Shia Islam.

jalabiya   Kaftan dress worn by women in both casual and formal settings.

jihad   Struggle against external or internal forces.

Kaaba   Holy shrine in Islam built around the Black Stone of Mecca; during hajj, pilgrims circumambulate it seven times.

kandoura   Full-length pullover dress worn by both men and women, although with a different style.

karma   Actions, good or bad, that when tabulated, influence how one's soul will be reborn in the next life; part of the Hindu belief system.

Khaleeji   Term meaning "Gulf" that references everything from the geographic area to its customs and language.

khanjar   Traditional dagger sheathed in a decorative and curved cover, worn by men around the waist.

Khariji   Sect of Ibadi Islam that believes Ali was an unworthy leader of Islam because of his compromise with a rival contender for leadership.

khitan   Circumcision.

khutba   Friday sermon.

lewa   A song and dance tradition sung in a combination of Arabic and Swahili.

madrassa A school, often religious, attached to or near a mosque.

mahr Bride-price; a gift from the groom to the bride on marriage.

majlis Formal meeting place, now used to denote a living room or parlor.

mihrab A niche in the mosque that faces Mecca and orients people during prayer.

muezzin A community member who calls people to prayer by chanting from an elevated place, often a tower of a mosque.

mujtahid Shiite religious leaders, guided by the imam.

niqab Facial veil worn with a *shayla* or other hair covering.

oud Pear-shaped, fretless string instrument that is the predecessor to the modern lute.

oryx Antelope found in the Gulf.

saggar Falcon trainer.

salat Second pillar of Islam, praying five times during the day.

sawm Fourth pillar of Islam, the practice of fasting during the holy month of Ramadan.

sawt Arabic blues musical genre influenced by African, Indian, and Persian music and centered in Kuwait and Bahrain.

shahada First pillar of Islam, proclamation and testament of faith.

Sharia Islamic law that governs all aspects of a Muslim's life.

shayla Scarf head covering that is a long rectangle of material.

Shia Sect of Islam known as the partisans of Ali, widely associated with Iran but with sizeable populations in the Gulf.

shisha Water pipe for smoking flavored and unflavored tobacco.

Sunna Guidelines for how to live one's life, based on the actions and sayings of the Prophet.

Sunni Sect of Islam that is known as the way of the Prophet (al-Sunna).

suq Marketplace.

tagiyah A small skullcap worn by men alone or under the *ghutra*.

thoub A tunic garment worn by men and women.

umma Community of believers (in Islam).

wadi Streambed or ravine between mountains.

Wahhabi Reformist movement within Sunni Islam that is more puritanical and linked to practices in the first three generations of Islam.

wasta System of influence and reciprocity that rests on family and personal connections and reputation.

wudu Washing one's head and feet before prayer; an ablution.

zakat Almsgiving, one of the pillars of Islam.

zar A form of healing ritual that includes dance.

Bibliography

Abu Saud, Abeer. *Qatari Women: Past and Present*. London: Longman Group Limited, 1984.

Adra, Najwa. "Dance in the Arabian Peninsula." In *The Garland Encyclopedia of World Music*, vol. 6, *The Middle East*, eds. Virginia Danielson, Scott Marcus, and Dwight Reynolds, 703–712. New York: Routledge, 1998.

Al-Fahim, Mohammed. *From Rags to Riches: A Story of Abu Dhabi*. London: London Centre of Arab Studies, 1995.

Al-Murr, Mohammad. *Dubai Tales*. Translated by Peter Clark. London: Forest Books, 1991.

———. *The Wink of the Mona Lisa*. Translated by Jack Briggs. Dubai: Motivate, 1994.

Al-Rasheed, Madawi, ed. *Transnational Connections and the Arab Gulf*. London: Routledge, 2005.

Al-Sanousi, Haifa, ed. *The Echo of Kuwaiti Creativity: A Collection of Translated Kuwaiti Short Stories*. Kuwait City: Centre for Research and Studies on Kuwait, 2001.

Al-Thakeb, Fahed. "The Arab Family and Modernity: Evidence from Kuwait." *Current Anthropology* 26, no. 5 (1985): 575–580.

Altoma, Salih J. *Modern Arabic Literature in Translation: A Companion*. London: Saqi Books, 2005.

Amaireh, Ali Hussein. "Color in the UAE Public Houses." *Journal of Architectural and Planning Research* 23, no. 1 (2006): 27–42.

Andersen, Richard, and Jawaher al-Bader. "Recent Kuwaiti Architecture: Regionalism vs. Globalization." *Journal of Architectural and Planning Research* 23, no. 2 (2006): 134–146.

Asfour, John Mikhail, trans. and ed. *When the Words Burn: An Anthology of Modern Arabic Poetry: 1945–1987*. Dunvegan, Ontario: Cormorant Books, 1988.

Badawi, M. M., ed. *Modern Arabic Literature*. Cambridge: Cambridge University Press, 1992.

Badley, Bill. "The Gulf and Yemen." In *World Music*, vol. 1, *Africa, Europe and the Middle East, the Rough Guide*, eds. Simon Broughton, Mark Ellingham, and Richard Trillo, 351–354. London: Rough Guides, 1999.

Bahrain: The Complete Residents' Guide. Dubai: Explorer, 2006.

Bahry, Louay, and Phebe Marr. "Qatari Women: A New Generation of Leaders?" *Middle East Policy* 12, no. 2 (2005): 104–119.

Barth, Fredrik. *Sohar: Culture and Society in an Omani Town*. Baltimore: Johns Hopkins University Press, 1983.

Bulloch, John. *The Persian Gulf Unveiled*. New York: Longdon & Weed, 1984.

Caesar, Judith. *Writing off the Beaten Track: Reflections on the Meaning of Travel and Culture in the Middle East*. Syracuse, NY: Syracuse University Press, 2002.

Campbell, Kay Hardy. "Women's Music of the Arabian Peninsula." In *The Garland Encyclopedia of World Music*, vol. 6, *The Middle East*, eds. Virginia Danielson, Scott Marcus, and Dwight Reynolds, 695–702. New York: Routledge, 1998.

Chatty, Dawn. "The Bedouin of Central Oman." *Journal of Oman Studies* 6, no. 1 (1983): 149–162.

———. *Mobile Pastoralists: Development Planning and Social Change in Oman*. New York: Columbia University Press, 1996.

———. "Women and Work in Oman: Cultural Constraints and Individual Choice." *International Journal of Middle East Studies* 32, no. 2 (2000): 241–254.

Christensen, Dieter. "Musical Life in Sohar, Oman." In *The Garland Encyclopedia of World Music*, vol. 6, *The Middle East*, eds. Virginia Danielson, Scott Marcus, and Dwight Reynolds, 671–683. New York: Routledge, 1998.

Clerk, Jayana, and Ruth Siegel, eds. *Modern Literatures of the Non-Western World: Where the Waters Are Born*. New York: HarperCollins, 1995.

Cohen-Mor, Dalya, ed. and trans. *An Arabian Mosaic: Short Stories by Arab Women Writers*. Potomac, MD: Sheba Press, 1993.

Crawford, Harriet. *Dilmun and Its Gulf Neighbours*. Cambridge: Cambridge University Press, 1998.

Crosese, Jaap. *Oman: A Pictorial Souvenir*. Dubai: Motivate, 2006.

Damluji, Salma Samar. *The Architecture of the United Arab Emirates*. Reading, UK: Garnet, 2006.

Davidson, Christopher. *The United Arab Emirates: A Study in Survival*. Boulder, CO: Lynne Rienner, 2005.

Davis, Mike. "Fear and Money in Dubai." *New Left Review* 41 (2006): 47–68.

Eickelman, Christine. *Women and Community in Oman*. New York: New York University Press, 1984.

———. "Women and Politics in an Arabian Oasis." In *A Way Prepared: Essays on Islamic Culture in Honour of Richard Bayly Winder*, eds. Farhad Kazemi and R. D. McChesney, 199–215. New York: New York University Press, 1988.

Eickelman, Dale F. "Omani Village: The Meaning of Oil." In *The Politics of Middle Eastern Oil*, ed. J. E. Peterson, 211–219. Washington, DC: Middle East Institute, 1983.

———. "From Theocracy to Monarchy: Authority and Legitimacy in Inner Oman, 1935–1957." *International Journal of Middle East Studies* 17, no. 1 (1985): 3–24.

El-Mallah, Issam, ed. *Omani Traditional Music and the Arab Heritage*. Tutzing, Germany: Hans Schneider, 2002.

Fagan, Peter. "An Introduction to the Traditional Architecture of the Arabian Peninsula." http://www.agmgifts.co.uk/resources/article.html.

Fairbairn, Anne, and Ghazi al-Gosaibi. *Feather and the Horizon: A Selection of Modern Poetry from across the Arab World*. Canberra, ACT: Leros Press, 1989.

Fakhro, Munira A. *Women at Work: A Case Study of Bahrain*. New York: Kegan Paul International, 1990.

Faqir, Fadia, ed. *In the House of Silence: Autobiographical Essays by Arab Women Writers*. Translated by Shirley Eber and Fadia Faqir. Reading, UK: Garnet, 1998.

Ferdinand, Klaus. *Bedouins of Qatar*. New York: Thames and Hudson, 1993.

Fox, John W., Nada Mourtada-Sabbah, and Mohammed al-Mutawa. "The Arab Gulf Region: Traditionalism Globalized or Globalization Traditionalized?" In *Globalization and the Gulf*, eds. John W. Fox, Nada Mourtada-Sabbah, and Mohammed al-Mutawa, 3–59. London: Routledge, 2006.

Gerrard, Mike, and Thomas McCarthy, eds. *Passport to Arabia*. Chippenham, England: Antony Rowe, 1993.

Gillespie, Frances. *Discovering Qatar*. Rimons, France: Creative Writing and Photography, 2006.

Graz, Liesl. *The Omanis: Sentinels of the Gulf*. London: Longman, 1982.

Handal, Nathalie, ed. *The Poetry of Arab Women: A Contemporary Anthology*. New York: Interlink Books, 2001.

Hawker, Ronald, Daniel Hull, and Omid Rouhani. "Wind-towers and Pearl Fishing: Architectural Signals in the Late Nineteenth and Early Twentieth Century Arabian Gulf." *Antiquity* 79, no. 305 (2005): 625–635.

Heard-Bey, Frauke. "The United Arab Emirates: Statehood and Nation-building in a Traditional Society." *The Middle East Journal* 59, no. 3 (2005): 357–375.

Held, Colbert. *Middle East Patterns: Places, Peoples, and Politics*. 4th ed. Boulder, CO: Westview Press, 2006.

Higgins, Kevin. *The Emirates*. Photographs by Hélène Rogers. Reading, UK: Garnet, 1995.

Hourani, Albert. *A History of the Arab Peoples*. New York: MJF Books, 1991.

Hurreiz, Sayyid Hamid. *Folklore and Folklife in the United Arab Emirates*. London: Routledge, 2002.

Jargy, Simon. "Sung Poetry in the Arabian Peninsula." In *The Garland Encyclopedia of World Music,* vol. 6, *The Middle East*, eds. Virginia Danielson, Scott Marcus, and Dwight Reynolds, 663–669. New York: Routledge, 1998.

Jayyusi, Salma Khadra, ed. *Short Arabic Plays: An Anthology*. New York: Interlink Books, 2003.

————. *Modern Arabic Poetry: An Anthology*. New York: Columbia University Press, 1987.

Jayyusi, Salma Khadra, and Roger Allen, eds. *Modern Arabic Drama: An Anthology*. Bloomington: Indiana University Press, 1995.

Kanafani, Aida. "Aesthetics and Ritual in the United Arab Emirates." PhD diss., University of Texas at Austin, 1983.

Kanna, Ahmed. "Dubai in a Jagged World." *Middle East Report Online* 243 (2007). http://www.merip.org/mer/mer243/kanna.html.

Keohane, Alan. *Bedouin: Nomads of the Desert*. London: Kyle Cathie, 2003.

Khalaf, Sulayman. "Gulf Societies and the Image of Unlimited Good." *Dialectical Anthropology* 17, no. 1 (1992): 53–84.

————. "Poetics and Politics of Newly Invented Tradition in the Gulf: Camel Racing in the United Arab Emirates." *Ethnology* 39, no. 3 (2000): 243–261.

Lambert, Jean. "The Arabian Peninsula: An Overview." In *The Garland Encyclopedia of World Music,* vol. 6, *The Middle East*, eds. Virginia Danielson, Scott Marcus, and Dwight Reynolds, 649–661. New York: Routledge, 1998.

Lancaster, William. *The Rwala Bedouin Today.* 2nd ed. Long Grove, IL: Waveland, 1997.

Landen, Robert G. "Oman." In *Encyclopedia of the Modern Middle East and North Africa,* 2nd ed., ed. Philip Mattar, 1709–1711. Detroit, MI: Macmillan Reference USA, 2004.

Lawson, Fred H. *Bahrain: The Modernization of Autocracy*. Boulder, CO: Westview Press, 1989.

————. "Bahrain." In *Encyclopedia of the Modern Middle East and North Africa,* 2nd ed., ed. Philip Mattar, 367–370. Detroit, MI: Macmillan Reference USA, 2004.

Leinhardt, Peter. *Shaikhdoms of Eastern Arabia*. Edited by Ahmed al-Shahi. Oxford: Palgrave, 2001.

Leonard, Karen. "South Asians in the Indian Ocean World: Language, Policing, and Gender Practices in Kuwait and the United Arab Emirates." *Comparative Studies of South Asia, Africa, and the Middle East* 25, no. 3 (2005): 677–686.

Lockerbie, John. "An Approach to Understanding Gulf Architecture." http://www.catnaps.org/islamic/gulfarch.html.

Longva, Anh Nga. "Nationalism in Pre-modern Guise: The Discourse of Hadhar and Badu in Kuwait." *International Journal of Middle East Studies* 38, no. 2 (2006): 171–187.

Marchal, Roland. "Dubai: Global City and Transnational Hub." In *Transnational Connections and the Arab Gulf,* ed. Madawi al-Rasheed, 93–110. London: Routledge, 2005.

"Marriage and Divorce, Emirates-Style." *The Economist* 358, no. 8206 (2001): 48.

Metz, Helen Chapin, ed. *Persian Gulf States: Country Studies*. 3rd ed. Washington, DC: Federal Research Division, Library of Congress, 1994.

Michalak-Pikulska, Barbara. *The Contemporary Kuwaiti Short Story in Peace Time and War 1929–1995*. Krakow, Poland: Enigma Press, 1998.

————. *Modern Poetry and Prose of Oman 1970–2000*. Krakow, Poland: Enigma Press, 2002.

————. "Literary Movement in the Gulf Countries." In *Authority, Privacy and Public Order in Islam*, eds. B. Michalak-Pikulska and A. Pikulski, 179–187. Leuven, Belgium: Peeters, 2004.

Miles, Hugh. *Al-Jazeera: The Inside Story of the Arab News Channel That Is Challenging the West*. New York: Grove Press, 2005.

Nagy, Sharon. "Social Diversity and Changes in the Form and Appearance of the Qatari House." *Visual Anthropology* 10 (1997): 281–304.

————. "'This Time I Think I'll Try a Filipina': Global and Local Influences on Relations between Foreign Household Workers and Their Employers in Doha, Qatar." *City & Society* 10, no. 1 (1998): 83–103.

————. "Dressing Up Downtown: Urban Development and Government Public Image in Qatar." *City & Society* 12, no. 1 (2000): 125–147.

————. "Making Room for Migrants, Making Sense of Difference: Spatial and Ideological Expressions of Social Diversity in Urban Qatar." *Urban Studies* 43, no. 1 (2006): 119–137.

Nydell, Margaret. *Understanding Arabs: A Guide for Modern Times.* Boston: Intercultural Press, 2006.

Obank, Margaret, and Samuel Shimon. *A Crack in the Wall: New Arab Poetry*. London: Saqi Books, 2001.

Oman: Residents' and Visitors' Guide. Dubai: Explorer, 2005.

Peck, Malcolm. "Kuwait." In *Encyclopedia of the Modern Middle East and North Africa*, 2nd ed., ed. Philip Mattar, 1347–1351. Detroit, MI: Macmillan Reference USA, 2004a.

————. "Qatar." In *Encyclopedia of the Modern Middle East and North Africa,* 2nd ed., ed. Philip Mattar, 1875–1878. Detroit, MI: Macmillan Reference USA, 2004b.

————. "United Arab Emirates." In *Encyclopedia of the Modern Middle East and North Africa,* 2nd ed., ed. Philip Mattar, 2269–2272. Detroit, MI: Macmillan Reference USA, 2004c.

Peterson, J. E. *Oman in the Twentieth Century: Political Foundations of an Emerging State*. London: Croom Helm, 1978.

————. "Legitimacy and Political Change in Yemen and Oman." *Orbis* 27, no. 4 (1984): 971–998.

————. "The Political Status of Women in the Arab Gulf States." *Middle East Journal* 43, no. 1 (1989): 34–50.

Piscatori, James, and Paul Dresch, eds. *Monarchies and Nations: Globalisation and Identity in the Arab States of the Gulf.* London: I. B. Tauris, 2005.

Ramsay, Gail. "Styles of Expression in Women's Literature in the Gulf." *Orientalia Suecana* 51–52 (2002–2003): 371–390.

————. "Confining the Guest-Laborers to the Realm of the Subaltern in Modern Literature from the Persian Gulf." *Orientalia Suecana* 53 (2004): 133–142.

————. "Symbolism and Surrealism in Literature from Bahrain." *Orientalia Suecana* 54 (2005): 133–150.

————. "Global Heroes and Local Characters in Short Stories from the United Arab Emirates and the Sultanate of Oman." *Middle Eastern Literatures* 9, no. 2 (2006a): 211–216.

————. "Globalisation and Cross-cultural Writing in the United Arab Emirates and the Sultanate of Oman." In *Literary History: Towards a Global Perspective,* vol. 4, *Literary Interactions in the Modern World 2*, ed. Stefan Helgesson, 241–277. Berlin: Walter de Gruyter, 2006b.

Rathmell, Andrew, and Kirsten Schulze. "Political Reform in the Gulf: The Case of Qatar." *Middle Eastern Studies* 36, no. 4 (2000): 47–62.

Rizvi, S.A.H., S.A.A. Naqvi, M. Hussain, and A. S. Hasan. "Religious Circumcision: A Muslim View." *BJU International* 83, suppl. 1 (1999): 13–16.

Rizzo, Helen, Katherine Meyer, and Yousef Ali. "Women's Political Rights: Islam, Status and Networks in Kuwait." *Sociology* 36, no. 3 (2002): 639–662.

Salloum, Habeeb. "Women in the United Arab Emirates." *Contemporary Review* 283 (2003): 101–104.

Scarce, Jennifer. *The Evolving Culture of Kuwait.* Edinburgh: HMSO, 1985.

Schvaneveldt, Paul, Jennifer Kerpelman, and Jay Schvaneveldt. "Generational and Cultural Changes in Family Life in the United Arab Emirates: A Comparison of Mothers and Daughters." *Journal of Comparative Family Studies* 36, no. 1 (2005): 77–91.

Seery, Gail. *Kuwait: A New Beginning.* Dubai: Motivate, 1993.

Seikaly, May. "Women and Social Change in Bahrain." *International Journal of Middle East Studies* 26, no. 3 (1994): 415–426.

Stratton, Allegra. "Women in Black Who Want to Vote." *New Statesman* 134, no. 4731 (2005): 10.

Strickert, Fred. "Christianity in the Gulf." *Washington Report on Middle East Affairs* (March 2000): 68, 71.

Tahboub, M. Daoud. *Short Story in the UAE.* Abu Dhabi, UAE: Ministry of Information and Culture, 2000.

Tetreault, Mary. "Autonomy, Necessity, and the Small State: Ruling Kuwait in the Twentieth Century." *International Organization* 45, no. 4 (1991): 565–591.

————. *Stories of Democracy: Politics and Society in Contemporary Kuwait.* New York: Columbia University Press, 2000.

Vine, Peter, and Paula Casey. *Kuwait: A Nation's Story.* London: Immel, 1992.

Wikan, Unni. *Behind the Veil in Arabia: Women in Oman.* Baltimore: Johns Hopkins University Press, 1982.

Wilkinson, John. *The Imamate Tradition of Oman.* Cambridge: Cambridge University Press, 1987.

Yarwood, John. "Al Muharraq: Architecture of a Traditional Arabian Town in Bahrain." *Arts and the Islamic World* 36 (2001): 3–82.

Zahlan, Rosemarie Said. *The Making of the Modern Gulf States: Kuwait, Bahrain, Qatar, the United Arab Emirates and Oman.* London: Unwin Hyman, 1989.

WEB SITES

Bahrain Guide, http://bahrainguide.org/.

Countries and Their Cultures, http://www.everyculture.com/.

Cultural Profiles Project, http://www.cp-pc.ca/.

Embassy of Qatar, Washington, D.C., http://www.qatarembassy.net/.

Islamic Architecture, http://www.islamicart.com/main/architecture/intro.html.

Kingdom of Bahrain, e-Government, http://www.e.gov.bh/wps/portal.

Ministry of Information, Sultanate of Oman, http://www.omanet.om/english/home.
    asp.

Office of the Emir of Kuwait, http://www.da.gov.kw/eng/.

Oman Centre for Traditional Music, http://www.octm-folk.gov.om/meng/
    musicology01.asp.

UAE Interact, http://www.uaeinteract.com/.

Index

About the Authors

REBECCA L. TORSTRICK is Associate Professor of Anthropology and Associate Dean of the College of Liberal Arts and Sciences at Indiana University, South Bend.

ELIZABETH FAIER is former Director of Sheikha Fatima Center for Leadership at Zayed University in Dubai. A cultural anthropologist by training, she is currently working as an independent scholar.